Girl to Girl:

60 Mother-Daughter Devotions for a Closer Relationship and Deeper Faith

Written by Tween-Daughter & Mother Coauthors

Bekah and Stacey Pardoe

ESTD 2016

YELLOW POPLAR

PRESS

Girl to Girl

Copyright © 2022 by Stacey Pardoe

Cover Design by Jaime Wiebel

"Calling all moms and daughters! I've got a wonderful new devotional to tell you about that's been created just for you—by a mom-and-daughter team. This book will encourage you and get you talking about inspirational topics. Ready to build a stronger bridge with your girl? Ready to add more laughter and significance to your relationship? You need to check out this new gem from Stacey and Bekah Pardoe."

Melanie Redd, author of the Best-Seller, *Live in Light*

"As the mom of six grown daughters, I always searched high and low for a devotional book that would be meaningful to my girls but would not cause awkward conversations or eye-rolling. Bekah and Stacey have written a delightful and relevant resource. This devotional is crafted in a way that opens doors to conversation and will cultivate deeper connections between moms and daughters. They portray a loving God who is able to do immeasurably more than we could ever ask or imagine. I highly recommend this encouraging resource and believe it will be a blessing to both mom and daughter alike."

Kelly Haux, children's pastor and director of family ministries at Grove City Alliance Church, 2006-2022

"Many moms and daughters are looking for deeper connections through faith-based conversations. In this delightful devotional, Stacey Pardoe and her daughter Bekah speak hope and encouragement into your bond as mother and daughter. This warm, engaging book will help you connect deeper with God while you build a stronger mother-daughter connection. It contains many talking points and prayer prompts to open up new conversations between moms and daughters."

Sarah Geringer, Christian author, speaker, podcaster, creative coach, and book launch manager at sarahgeringer.com

"Stacey and Bekah are an inspiration. I love their honesty and godly wisdom on topics that touch women and girls of every age. Their questions are perfect conversation starters. And my favorite part is that they want this to be a fun way for mothers and daughters to grow closer to each other as they are growing closer to the Lord."

Deb Wolf, author and writer at CountingMyBlessings.com

To mothers and daughters of all ages,

you are loved so much more than you can imagine.

Table of Contents

Welcome to the Conversation!

Welcome to *Girl to Girl*! We're thrilled you're here. We hope to make you laugh, help you grow closer to each other, and help you both grow in your faith. I'm Stacey (the Mom), and Bekah is my sixth-grade daughter. We had a blast writing this book together, and we can't wait to share our hearts with you.

Many mother-daughter devotionals exist, but this one is unique because it includes writing by a girl your age. Bekah knows all about the situations you face every day because she faces them too. She offers input into everything from how to handle an unwanted crush to dealing with jealousy within friendships.

As you join us on this journey, we hope you will imagine we're on a mother-daughter ice cream date. Imagine we're sitting across the table from you with our brownie batter ice cream cones as we talk about God, school, relationships, and life. We invite you to join in the conversation, share your hearts, and connect with God and each other through this process.

We believe God wants to use this devotional to bless your relationship and draw you deeper into his love. We'll tell you more about ourselves shortly. First, we want to tell you how this book came to be, what to expect, and how to use it!

How This Book Came to Be: Bekah's Brilliant Idea

The inspiration for this book was birthed when Bekah noticed a mother-daughter devotional on our kitchen table. She approached me and excitedly said, "Mom, we should write a mother-daughter devotional book together!"

I thought it was a great idea, but I also expected the enthusiasm to fade within a few days. Instead, Bekah insisted we start writing. Not one to stifle my girl's dreams, we brainstormed a short list of topics. I wrote a few devotions and asked her to add her input. Bekah immediately got to work, and I realized she was serious about the project. Since that day, we've been working hard to compile a relevant, Spirit-breathed, practical devotional book to inspire mothers and daughters.

Our vision is two-fold: First, we hope these devotions will help you grow closer to one another as mother and daughter. Second, we hope you are challenged to grow closer to God as you enjoy him together.

What to Expect

Within these pages, you'll find 60 devotions. Each devotion will take about five minutes to read and a few more minutes to discuss (depending on how chatty you are—and we encourage you to chat it up!).

You might read these devotions together in the mornings, before bed, or at any time of day that works for your schedule. Find a time when the two of you can share your hearts in privacy—away from the noise of other family members like noisy little siblings. Make it a special "Girl Time" to look forward to. This isn't one more item to add to a full to-do list. It's an opportunity to slip away and grow together while growing in your faith.

There's no timeline for reading the 60 devotions within the book. Use the devotional as often as your schedule allows. You might read it every day, twice a week, or only at a designated time over the weekend. Go at your own pace. There is no hurry. Consider this book an invitation to enjoy God and enjoy one another.

We wrote this book thinking of the issues faced by girls ages 10 through 15; however, the topics discussed could be used for moms and daughters of any age. Most of the devotions are applicable regardless of age. If you are 80 and your daughter is 50, we welcome you! Mom, you might need to offer additional explanations for some of the devotions if your daughter is younger than eight, but feel free to read it with a younger daughter as well.

Additionally, we'd like to point out that this is not a devotional exclusively for biological mothers and daughters. It could be used between a grandma and granddaughter, an aunt and a niece, an older sister and a younger sister, or an older mentor and younger friend.

How to Use This Devotional

Each devotion in this book begins with a verse cited from the New International Version of Scripture, a commentary from Stacey (called "Mom's Thoughts"), a commentary from Bekah (called "Girl to Girl"), several discussion questions, a prayer, and a journaling section.

As we mentioned, we encourage you to read the devotional out loud together in a peaceful place and take your time responding to the discussion questions together. Don't be afraid to venture off-topic and follow wherever the conversation leads if the discussion questions prompt a different topic.

Remember that the goal for this time is to connect with one another while connecting with God. This journey is an opportunity to grow closer to each other. Keep this in mind if you disagree on certain issues. Agree to disagree if there is no clear-cut answer. You are here to enjoy one another.

Lastly, the "Journal Later" section at the end of each devotion provides space to step away and further reflect on the day's reading by responding to a final writing prompt in your own time. You will find designated areas for each of you to write your reflections.

Bekah came up with the idea for this section after enjoying a mother-daughter-shared journal we worked on together. The journal we share prompts us each to write about a specific topic, and we pass the journal back and forth. When Bekah is finished, she leaves the journal on my bed. When I finish, I leave the journal in her room. We take turns passing it back and forth without hurrying or pressuring one another. It's a fun way to communicate.

We encourage you to follow a similar sequence. After finishing your devotional time, one of you can volunteer to write in the journal first. It doesn't matter who writes first. When the first writer is finished, leave the journal in a designated place. Again, we want you to enjoy this process. If you're not into journaling, don't get hung up on it. Remember that this isn't about rules— it's about connection.

Have Fun

Lastly, we encourage you to have fun with this book. Laugh often. Don't take yourselves or your opinions too seriously. We did our best to anchor our readings in the Word of God and honor God while also letting our personalities shine through the readings! We hope you enjoy your time with us, and we are deeply honored you are here.

Before we begin, we'll tell you a little bit about ourselves because we hope to connect with you as friends in this space.

About Us

Remember, we're imagining we're on a mother-daughter ice cream date right now! We're sitting across the picnic table from you, and we both have chocolate ice cream awkwardly smeared across our chins.

Bekah is looking cute in her new denim jacket and ripped jeans. Because I'm a sporty mom, I'm wearing my favorite baseball cap and a hoodie. Got the image?! Great! Let us tell you about ourselves!

Bekah: Well, like most girls my age, I like to hang out with my friends. I also like snacks (giggling), and I like to do anything artistic. I run cross-country and helped coach my brother's soccer team in the spring. Right now, I want to be a pediatric nurse when I grow up. I also love caring for animals. I have four large reptile tanks in my bedroom!

Mom: Thanks, babe. As for me, I used to be a high school special education teacher, but after Bekah and her two little brothers came along, I became a full-time mom. I'm a blogger, author, and freelance writer. I like to run, hike, and do anything outside. I think that's all you need to know for now!

Bekah: WAIT!!!! We didn't tell them about the boys—or the pets! My dad's name is Darrell, and he works as a forester. From this point forward, we will call him the Lumberjack (You're welcome, Dad!).

I also have an eight-year-old brother named Caleb. Recently, he's been into searching for "treasures" with his new metal detector. My youngest brother is named Aiden. He's three and likes monster trucks, puddles, and lollipops.

We also have a few pets. I have a leopard gecko, a bearded dragon, and an aquarium with fish in my room. Outside, we have three beagles and a quail!

That sums it up. You'll learn more about us in the pages to come! Let's get started!

Who Are You?

And I pray that you, being rooted and established in love, may have power, together with all the Lord's holy people, to grasp how wide and long and high and deep is the love of Christ.

Ephesians 3:17-18

Mom's Thoughts:

If I asked you to describe yourself with one word, what would you say?

When I was younger, I often described myself as athletic, creative, and hard-working. Sometimes, I described myself by my hobbies and talents. Other times, I answered this question with the word *determined*. I was determined to get good grades and excel at sports.

Determination served me well until something extremely difficult happened. I got sick—*terribly* sick—and the sickness lasted close to a year. I was so sick that I could barely get out of bed, and when I tried to push through the sickness, it got worse. Determination was totally failing me!

During those long months, every label I had used to define me was stripped away. I wasn't able to be a good friend or daughter. I couldn't run, hike, or even sit up on the couch! It felt like my identity had been taken from me.

A few months into the illness, God showed me a truth that changed my life forever. He showed me the one part of my identity that can never be taken away from me: I will always be loved by him. Every other part of my identity can change—my talents, hobbies, relationships, and physical capabilities can change—but I will always be God's beloved daughter.

This is true for you too. You might describe yourself by the activities you enjoy, your appearance, or your talents; however, all of these parts of you are subject to change. Only one part of your identity can never change: You are unconditionally loved by God, and his love can never be taken away from you!

Girl to Girl:

Our family lives by three main values, and these values are framed on our kitchen wall. The first value is to remember we are loved and cherished by God. God doesn't care what we look like or what flaws we have. He loves us just the way we are. This is the truest thing about each of us.

Our family's second value is to always be kind, and our third value is to give our best effort at all times. It's important to be kind and work hard, but if we don't remember that we are loved and cherished by God first, we might think that what we do is more important than who we are!

God wants you to know you are loved by him, and his love cannot be taken away from you. Remember this the next time someone asks you to describe yourself!

Talk About It:

- Before reading today's devotion, what would you have said if someone asked you to describe yourself with one word? Is it possible that this word might no longer describe you in the future?

- Has God ever taken away something that felt like part of your identity? Maybe you had to quit playing a sport you loved or got sick for a long time and couldn't do much at all. How can you find strength in future times of loss by remembering you are God's beloved daughter?

Pray Together:

Lord, thank you that your love can never be taken away from us. Help us grasp the depth of your love on a deeper level today. Empower us to live from our unchanging identities as your beloved daughters. Amen.

Journal Later:

If you could describe yourself using three words, what words would you use? Share your reasons for choosing each of these three words. Remember this: Even if these words don't describe you in the future, you will always be God's *beloved* daughter.

Mom's Reflection:

_____

_____

_____

_____

_____

_____

_____

_____

_____

_____

_____

_____

_____

_____

_____

_____

Daughter's Reflection:

_____

_____

_____

_____

_____

_____

_____

_____

_____

_____

_____

_____

_____

What If . . .

Surely God is my salvation; I will trust and not be afraid.

Isaiah 12:2

Mom's Thoughts:

I'll never forget my first day of sixth grade. Throughout the previous six years of elementary school, I went to a tiny school with the same group of classmates every year. We were as close as siblings, and starting school was never scary because we knew each other so well.

Sixth grade was different.

In sixth grade, we started middle school at a much larger school with hundreds of other students. I was nervous about getting lost, making friends, opening the lock on my locker, and a million different "what-if" scenarios.

You might feel nervous about a what-if scenario in your life too. Maybe you're nervous about moving to a new house, starting a new sport, getting sick, getting lost, or going away to summer camp. If you're like me, you know how it feels to lie in bed at night and rehearse potential what-if scenarios.

A few years ago, a friend helped me work through a challenging what-if scenario I was facing. She asked, "Would God still be good if this situation went as horribly as possible? Could you trust him to walk with you through it?"

It took me a few weeks of wrestling with the question, but I finally realized that I could trust God's goodness—even if my worst-case scenario became reality. From that day forward, I found peace with my what-if situation.

God wants to help you trust him with your what-if scenarios too. You might not trust him yet. That's okay. Pray a prayer that goes like this: "God, I want to trust you. Please help me trust you more." God will answer this prayer. As your trust grows, peace will begin to push out the anxiety you feel.

As for my middle school experience, it turned out just fine. I made lots of new friends, never got lost, and loved decorating my new locker! I also learned a valuable lesson: Most of our what-if scenarios never even take place. God wants us to throw off our worries and trust him to care for us.

Girl to Girl:

A few years ago, both of our pet dogs died within a few months. Around that time, I also lost my great-grandma. A couple of years later, my other great-grandma died. It was a hard time for me. I started to think, "I wonder what terrible thing is going to happen next!"

We all face times when the future feels scary. In these times, God is with us, teaching us how to trust him. It's helpful to remember this when we look ahead and feel afraid. Even if the worst what-if scenario happens, God will never leave us. He helps us and carries us.

After losing our dogs and both of my great-grandmas, God taught me that no matter how difficult life becomes, he will help me and guide me. He will help you face your future too. You can trust him!

Talk About It:

- What is your worst what-if scenario right now? How often do you think about this possible situation?
- Remember that even if this scenario happens, God will be with you, and he will help you. He will also show you what you need to do to get through it. What is he showing you about this scenario today? Do you need to ask him to help you grow in trust?

Pray Together:

Father, it's not always easy to trust you with our futures. We imagine terrible scenarios, and we are gripped by fear. Help us to trust that you always go before us and that you go with us into every situation. Amen.

Journal Later:

Describe a time in the past when you felt nervous or afraid about trying something new. Maybe you were having your first sleepover with a friend, going to summer camp, or starting a new school year. In what ways did God provide for you and help you?

Mom's Reflection:

_____

_____

_____

_____

_____

_____

_____

_____

_____

_____

_____

_____

_____

_____

_____

_____

_____

Daughter's Reflection:

_____

_____

_____

_____

_____

_____

_____

_____

_____

_____

_____

_____

Ditch the Drama!

Love does not dishonor others, it is not self-seeking, it is not easily angered, it keeps no record of wrongs.

1 Corinthians 13:5

Mom's Thoughts:

Do you have a friend who always seems to be mad at you? She might constantly tell you that you hurt her feelings or complain that you never have time for her. She gets jealous when you spend time with other friends, and you feel like you have to walk on eggshells when you're with her.

On the other hand, maybe you frequently confront your friends for hurting your feelings. You might feel jealous when your closest friend hangs out with her other friends. Maybe you feel like you put all the work into a certain friendship, and you often feel upset because your friend doesn't reach out to you in the same way.

Regardless of which scenario best describes you, let me share a powerful secret for healthy, thriving friendships: Hold your friends loosely.

You can be a good friend by offering love, a listening ear, compassion, and a place for fun. You can also be a good friend by giving your friends space.

Part of becoming mature is learning to extend grace and let it go when your friends fail to meet your expectations. Every hurt feeling doesn't have to become a hard conversation. Remind yourself that it's healthy for your friends to have a variety of different friends and ask God to help you overcome feelings of jealousy. Hold your friends loosely, and they will want to spend time with you.

Girl to Girl:

My mom sometimes reminds me to hold my friends with an open hand. This is good advice for us all.

You hold your friends with an open hand when you let them hang out with others and don't cause fights or create drama. You hold them with an open hand when you forgive them for letting you down. Everyone makes mistakes, and your friends will eventually let you down. Don't hold it against them. Instead, forgive them and move on.

It's also important to remember that friendships change over time. You might be close with a certain friend one year, but the next year, you are in different classes and drift apart. That's okay. Drifting closer together and then farther apart is natural in all friendships. Keep your heart open as your friends flow in and out of your inner circle.

Most importantly, give your friends space. Give them room to have other friends, change, and grow. Try not to become jealous when your friends spend time with others. It's okay to have a best friend, but try to remain open to having other friends as well. Friendships are always healthiest when we hold them loosely.

Talk About It:

- Do you have any friends who often seem upset with you? Why do they get upset, and how does it make you feel?
- Do you ever feel jealous of your friends? What is God showing you about these feelings in light of today's reading?
- In what ways might you need to hold your friendships more loosely and extend more grace?

Pray Together:

Lord, thank you for our friends. We want to learn how to be good friends to others. Help us hold our friends loosely and be patient with them. Help us avoid jealousy and extend the same kindness we hope to receive from others. Amen.

Journal Later:

Friends are an important part of our lives. God designed us to live in community with others and to find joy and growth through relationships. Describe your closest friend (or friends). What do you appreciate about this friend, and what makes this person a good friend to you?

Mom's Reflection:

_____

_____

_____

_____

_____

_____

_____

_____

_____

_____

_____

_____

_____

_____

_____

_____

Daughter's Reflection:

_____

_____

_____

_____

_____

_____

_____

_____

_____

_____

_____

_____

High-Low

You have searched me, Lord, and you know me. You know when I sit and when I rise; you perceive my thoughts from afar.

Psalm 139:1-2

Mom's Thoughts:

How do you cope with feelings of sadness and stress at the end of a bad day? Talking to a loved one (like your mom) and talking to God can help you process the hard parts of your days.

Bekah and I sometimes do an activity called "High-Low." At the end of the day, we share our happiest moments of the day as well as our toughest moments. We always feel a bit better after reflecting on our best moments. Talking about the difficult moments is helpful too. Opening up about the tough moments often feels like lifting a heavy burden.

High-Low is a great activity to share as mother and daughter, but we can also share our high and low moments with God. He is always listening and wants to help us sort through the hard parts of our days. He also wants to celebrate the good moments with us.

At the end of each day, I like to quiet myself with the Lord and review my best and worst moment. I ask God to show me one blessing from my day, and I savor the memory with him. I then ask him to show me a difficult moment, and I talk about it with him. I always feel a deep sense of peace after this time with the Lord.

Do you have any buried feelings that need to be let out? Try the High-Low activity with God tonight. Celebrating your good moments and talking to him about your difficult moments will help you feel lighter. God wants to carry your burdens and give you peace.

Girl to Girl:

Emotions can have a strong impact on our lives. Letting ourselves feel our emotions is important. It's okay to feel sad if someone hurts your feelings or a loved one lets you down. It's also healthy to talk about your feelings with someone you trust.

About a year ago, my mom was cleaning my turtle tank, and the tank shattered. I was very disappointed and sad because the turtles had to live in a plastic tub until we could find a bigger tank. After cleaning up all the water, we talked about my emotions. I realized it was okay to feel sad. I felt so much better after talking about my disappointment with my mom.

God also wants us to talk to him when we feel upset. We can talk to God the same way we talk to our friends. He is always listening and waiting to help us. When he speaks, his words always help heal our hearts.

As for the broken turtle tank, don't worry. We eventually found a new tank and solved the problem!

Talk About It:

- How often do you talk to God about the hard parts of your day? What stops you from bringing him your difficult moments?
- Right now, try the High-Low activity together. Share a good moment and a difficult moment from your day. This is a great time to talk about what's on your heart and encourage one another! (We encourage you to do this more often!)

Pray Together:

God, thank you for helping us navigate our difficult moments. Help us remember to turn to you as we deal with the difficult parts of our lives. We know you understand every difficult emotion we feel because you humbled yourself and lived on this Earth too. Thank you for stepping into a human body and feeling our pain. Your love and compassion amaze us! Amen.

Journal Later:

Try the High-Low activity individually as you reflect on the past week. Write about your best moment and your most difficult moment from the week. Notice the way you feel after taking a few minutes to reflect.

Mom's Reflection:

_____

_____

_____

_____

_____

_____

_____

_____

_____

_____

_____

_____

_____

_____

_____

_____

Daughter's Reflection:

_____

_____

_____

_____

_____

_____

_____

_____

_____

_____

_____

The Last Word

Pride goes before destruction, a haughty spirit before a fall.

Proverbs 16:18

Mom's Thoughts:

A few years ago, God convicted me of an ugly sin in my life. He showed me that I like to be right.

"I don't think so, God," I told him. "I'm just positive that I'm humble and teachable."

Despite my objections, God began to show me that I consistently tried to win arguments, have the last word, and prove myself to others. Soon, I caught myself bickering with my husband over where to park the lawn mower. The next day, I realized I was trying too hard to prove my point to a friend. I realized God was right: I like to be right!

Pride hides at the root of needing to prove ourselves, have the last word, and win arguments. We feel good about ourselves for being wise, and we put our need to prove ourselves above God's commands to love others and extend kindness.

If you have siblings, you probably know all about the desire to prove yourself. Your little brother spouts off some ridiculous fact about golden retrievers or cumulous clouds, and it feels oh-so-satisfying to jump in and correct him. Or maybe your dad is clueless when it comes to your favorite series on Netflix, and you feel proud when you correct his misspoken words or roll your eyes over his ridiculous questions.

Winning arguments and proving that we are right (and others are wrong) can feel good inside. However, it's important to remember that being kind is always more important than proving ourselves or having the last word.

Girl to Girl:

My brother and I used to bicker A LOT! We still do, but not nearly as much. He used to start making weird nonsense noises, and I would say, "Stop!"

He would say something like, "You're not Mom, and you can't make me do anything!"

"Yes, I can!" I would yell.

"No, you can't!" he would respond.

And on and on it would go.

Now, I see how silly it was to fight over such things. When he starts making weird noises, I try to calmly say, "Please stop."

Sometimes, he doesn't stop. I've learned that the best thing to do is ignore him or walk away. If I don't overreact, he eventually gives it up.

You might feel annoyed by someone in your family at times too. Remember this: Competing to have the last word will only create stress and chaos. Sometimes, the best thing to do is smile and walk away. Like my mom often says, "It's better to be kind to each other than to prove that you're right."

Talk About It:

- Ask the Lord to bring to mind a recent situation in which you needed to prove yourself, have the last word, win an argument, or be right about something. What was happening in this situation?
- Do you catch yourself trying to defend your views in a way that hurts others? What does God want to show you about your desire to prove yourself to others?

Pray Together:

Jesus, thank you for providing the ultimate demonstration of a life with nothing to prove. You often kept silent when others spoke against you. You didn't need to win arguments or have the last word. Your actions spoke louder than your words, and everything you did was in love. Help us follow your example as we lay down our desires to prove ourselves and, instead, aim to be loving. Amen.

Journal Later:

Describe a time when you caught yourself trying to prove something or trying to win an argument that didn't really matter. How might you respond differently next time?

Mom's Reflection:

_____

_____

_____

_____

_____

_____

_____

_____

_____

_____

_____

_____

_____

_____

_____

_____

_____

Daughter's Reflection:

_____

_____

_____

_____

_____

_____

_____

_____

_____

_____

_____

Feeling Alone

For the Spirit God gave us does not make us timid, but gives us power, love and self-discipline.

2 Timothy 1:7

Mom's Thoughts:

Have you ever felt lonely even though you were surrounded by people? Maybe you walked into a crowded classroom, looked for a place to sit, and everyone seemed to have a friend—everyone except you. It doesn't matter whether you're walking into a classroom for the first time or trying to find a place to belong at summer camp. It's entirely possible to be surrounded by cheerful people but feel dismal and alone.

Did you know there's a cure for this kind of loneliness?

Here is the cure: Instead of waiting for someone to reach out to you in a gesture of friendship, take the first step. Every time you walk into a crowded room, ask God to show you someone who needs his love and encouragement. Instead of looking for someone to help you fit in, focus on finding someone who might need encouragement. I've learned that every situation improves when I stop pondering what others are thinking about me and, instead, ask God to show me someone who needs an encounter with his love.

Reaching out to others can feel awkward, especially if you're shy, but the world is filled with people who are hungry for love and connection. Ask God to help you shift your focus away from yourself and start a conversation with one new person sometime this week. You might be surprised by where God leads you.

Girl to Girl:

Last summer, I went to summer camp for the first time. It was very awkward when I first walked into the cabin where I was staying. Some girls were lying in bed and resting while others were laughing with each other. I had a friend with me, but I still felt kind of lonely. I wondered if I would fit in.

Most of us feel lonely or feel like we don't fit in from time to time. One way to feel better is to just give it time. Usually, with time, you start to feel better and more settled. Another idea is to look for someone who might need a friend. Instead of thinking about who will make you feel included, go find a new friend. In most situations, someone else is feeling just as lonely and insecure as you feel. Ask God to lead you to these people and reach out in friendship.

As for my first year at summer camp, it took a day or two to settle in, but once I adjusted, I had a great time! Hang in there if you are adjusting to a new school or new situation. Give it time, look for someone to encourage, and God will help you feel more confident.

Talk About It:

- Have you ever felt awkward and alone even though you were surrounded by people? How did you react?
- When you walk into a crowded place where you don't know anyone, what is the first thought that usually comes into your mind? In what ways would these situations be different if you stopped looking for people to include you and, instead, looked for someone in need of a friend?
- Within the next week, what social situation might present an opportunity to reach out and connect with someone new by starting a conversation?

Pray Together:

Lord, thank you that because you love us, we don't need to try to fit into crowds or be accepted by others. Help us walk into new situations watching for other people who need your love. Help us stop looking inward and start looking outward. Amen.

Journal Later:

Share a memory from a time when someone else made you feel loved and included in a new situation. How can you pass this gift along to someone else?

Mom's Reflection:

_____

_____

_____

_____

_____

_____

_____

_____

_____

_____

_____

_____

_____

_____

_____

_____

Daughter's Reflection:

_____

_____

_____

_____

_____

_____

_____

_____

_____

_____

_____

_____

_____

_____

The Living Word

Your word, Lord, is eternal; it stands firm in the heavens.

Psalm 119:89

Mom's Thoughts:

Did you know that God wants to speak to you? God can speak in many ways, but one of the most reliable ways God speaks is through the Bible. I'll never forget the day God spoke to me through the Bible as an airplane carried me thousands of miles from my home and family.

I was 16 the first time I flew on an airplane. Waving goodbye to my parents, I walked onto the plane and headed to Wyoming for a week-long wilderness school.

A million worries rushed through my mind. I was worried about getting homesick, worried the food would be terrible, worried my luggage wouldn't arrive, and worried I wouldn't make any friends.

As I clicked my seatbelt and leaned back in the comfy chair, a Bible verse came to mind: "Therefore I tell you, do not worry about your life, what you will eat or drink; or about your body, what you will wear. Is not life more than food, and the body more than clothes?" (Matthew 6:25). I'd memorized the verse a few months earlier, and I knew Jesus was gently reminding me that he would care for me.

Jesus wants to speak to you through the Bible too. The Bible offers direction for our lives and wisdom to help us overcome our daily struggles. We're going to invite you to listen to God through the Bible at the end of this devotion. First, Bekah wants to describe a time when our evening Bible reading spoke straight to her heart.

Girl to Girl:

A few years ago, I saw a frightening commercial before bedtime, and I was so scared!!!! I told my mom I was feeling afraid, and we talked about how the commercial was pretend. But I still felt scared.

Well, every night, my mom read to me from a kids' Bible. That night, she flipped to the next page of the Bible to read our reading for the night. Sure enough, there was a verse about not being afraid! I was happy, and my mom told me that the verse was God's way of speaking to me.

That night, I wasn't scared when I went to sleep because God had talked to me and comforted me. If you open up your Bible, you might find something that feels like it's just for you. This is one way God talks to us! Isn't that exciting?

Talk About It:

- Has a Bible verse ever spoken directly into a situation you were facing? If not, we encourage you to make it a habit to read just a small portion of your Bible every day. You might be surprised by how often God's Word relates to your circumstances.
- Read Psalm 23 out loud together. As you read, listen for a word or phrase that catches your attention. (You might need to read it a second time as you watch for a phrase that seems to stand out to you.) After sharing the phrase that caught your attention, talk about how this phrase might be relevant to a situation you are facing in your life right now. What might God want to show you?

Pray Together:

Lord God, thank you for giving us your Word. Thank you for wanting to speak to us, spend time with us, and direct us. Please help us make time in your Word a priority. We want to hide it in our hearts and allow it to become the light that guides our lives. Amen.

Journal Later:

Have you ever sensed that God was speaking to you or showing you something? Share your experience right here. If you've never had this experience, describe a situation in your life in which you'd like to hear from God. What question would you ask him about this situation?

Mom's Reflection:

_____

_____

_____

_____

_____

_____

_____

_____

_____

_____

_____

_____

_____

_____

_____

_____

Daughter's Reflection:

_____

_____

_____

_____

_____

_____

_____

_____

_____

_____

_____

_____

_____

_____

Bogged Down

Cast your cares on the Lord and he will sustain you; he will never let the righteous be shaken.

Psalm 55:22

Mom's Thoughts:

Have you ever been worried about something that felt like it was bogging you down? Maybe you argued with a friend or failed a big test at school. Perhaps it was an even bigger problem: A loved one was sick or your parents were going through a divorce.

These are some heavy burdens. The Bible tells us to cast these cares on the Lord. You might be wondering what it looks like to cast your cares on the Lord. How do we cast our cares on God when we can't see him sitting with us face-to-face?

First, it might help to notice that this verse isn't telling us to gently lift our cares; we're supposed to *throw* them. God knows how heavy our burdens feel, and he wants us to robustly cast them onto him—even when we feel like we're being crushed.

You might feel too weak to cast your heavy burden onto the Lord, but I have good news. When the burden is too heavy to cast, God will lift it for you. All you need to do is ask him.

God is big enough to reach down and take your burdens from you. When I feel bogged down with a heavy burden, I imagine myself holding out the burden in my open hands. I then ask God to reach down and take it. I imagine him lifting the weight of my distress, and I trust that he has lifted my burden. I don't always feel relieved immediately, but every time the burden comes back into my mind, I remind myself that I already gave it to God.

Girl to Girl:

Sometimes, I feel stressed or worried. When I feel this way, I usually say a quick prayer. It's as easy as saying, "God, please help me to feel better." Usually, I feel a bit calmer after asking God for help.

It can be hard to give God your stress and your worries. Stress can linger inside you like a virus that eats away at you. When this happens, it's usually helpful to talk to an adult. A parent, teacher, grandparent, or any trusted adult will be happy to pray over you or try to help. Don't be afraid to ask.

You can also do things to keep your mind off of the stress. You might invite a friend to hang out or do something exciting to get your mind off the hard times. Most of all, remember that God wants you to bring your burdens to him. He is strong enough to lift even the heaviest burdens and help you feel lighter.

Talk About It:

- What heavy burden came to mind as you read today's devotion?
- What's stopping you from casting your heavy burden onto God?
- Try the activity described together today: Name your heaviest burden or biggest worry, hold it out in your open hands, and imagine God reaching down and lifting it. Every time you feel tempted to dwell on this issue in the future, remind yourself that you have entrusted it to God.

Pray Together:

God, thank you for the promise to carry our burdens for us. Thank you that your yoke is easy and your burden is light. Help us trust you to take our heaviest burdens and work behind the scenes in our lives. Amen.

Journal Later:

Is there a part of your life that frequently causes stress and worry? Maybe you worry about your grades, your friendships, your future, or something about you that makes you feel different from others. Write about this burden here today as a way of being open with one another and fulfilling God's command to carry one another's burdens.

Mom's Reflection:

_____

_____

_____

_____

_____

_____

_____

_____

_____

_____

_____

_____

_____

_____

_____

_____

Daughter's Reflection:

_____

_____

_____

_____

_____

_____

_____

_____

_____

_____

_____

_____

_____

_____

_____

_____

Your Biggest Messes

The Lord is gracious and compassionate, slow to anger and rich in love.

Psalm 145:8

Mom's Thoughts:

When I was younger, I imagined Jesus was similar to a grumpy king. I envisioned him looking down on me from heaven with disappointment in his eyes and a frown on his face.

I knew he was perfect and holy, and I didn't believe I was worthy of his love. My life was filled with sins like fighting with my older sister, telling white lies, and bickering with friends. I thought I needed to become godlier, pray more often, and read my Bible more regularly before I was worthy of Jesus' love.

Here's what I wish I would have known: Jesus doesn't look down on us from heaven with a grumpy expression on his face. He takes sin seriously, but he doesn't shame us for messing up either. He loves us more than we could ever fathom and wants to help us live with joy and hope.

Jesus isn't asking us to shape up or pull ourselves together. Instead, he invites us to turn to him in our messy, sinful, broken moments and let *him* do the work of setting us free and healing us. This is grace. Jesus pours his grace upon us when he works in our lives to accomplish what we cannot do for ourselves.

You might feel like your life is too big of a mess for Jesus to love you. Maybe you think you need to become a better person, break your bad habits, and start praying more often before you draw close to the Lord.

Jesus has an invitation for you today. He wants you to run to him just as you are, and *he* will help you live a joy-filled, vibrant life through the power of his love. He already took the punishment you deserve when he died on the cross for your sins. The price has been paid.

Jesus can handle your biggest troubles and dirtiest messes. He wants to help you sort through it.

He waits with open arms. We'll talk about how to surrender our lives to Jesus in the next devotion. Stay tuned—you don't want to miss it!

Girl to Girl:

Wow, Mom, are you saying I'm a mess?

My mom does have a point. None of us are perfect; however, it's important to realize that we don't have to be perfect for Jesus to accept us. He loves us just the way we are—messes and all!

Jesus wants you to turn to him and ask him to be the leader of your life. He wants to help you, heal you, and transform you with his love. He knows everything about you, and he loves you more than you could ever imagine.

You don't need to shape up, read your Bible more often, or quit your bad habits before you ask Jesus to help you and guide you. He is waiting to help you and guide you at this very moment!

Talk About It:

- Have you ever felt like you needed to be a better person for Jesus to accept and embrace you? Which parts of your life feel too messy to invite Jesus into?

- How will you respond to Jesus' invitation to run to him in the middle of your messy life?

Pray Together:

Jesus, thank you for inviting us to come to you in the middle of our messiest moments. None of us are perfect, and we all need you. Thank you for waiting for us with open arms and promising to help pull us from our messes. Amen.

Journal Later:

If you could ask Jesus to help you in one messy or broken area of your life, which area would you pick, and what would you want Jesus to do for you?

Mom's Reflection:

_____

_____

_____

_____

_____

_____

_____

_____

_____

_____

_____

_____

_____

_____

_____

_____

Daughter's Reflection:

_____

_____

_____

_____

_____

_____

_____

_____

_____

_____

_____

_____

_____

Jesus' Great Gift

Jesus answered, "I am the way and the truth and the life. No one comes to the Father except through me."

John 14:6

Mom's Thoughts:

I was 14 years old the first time I read John 14:6. My grandpa had passed away, and I took my Bible to a field behind my parents' house. I was determined to make sure I would go to heaven when I died.

Until that day, I believed that everyone who pursued religion in any form was on one of many paths to the same God. I believed that all the good people in this world would ultimately end up in heaven. The idea that there was only one way to God seemed far too limited.

Jesus' words in John 14:6 caught me off guard. He claimed to be the only way to access God and the only way to get to heaven. His words showed me that I could not claim to follow Jesus while believing there are many paths to God.

God used these words to call me into a relationship with Jesus that summer in the hayfield. As I read more of my Bible, I realized that we have all fallen short of God's perfect standards. We all deserve God's punishment. God's punishment is eternal suffering in hell, but his punishment also includes separation from him while we live on Earth.

Jesus died on the cross to take the punishment we deserve. Because of Jesus, we can have the assurance that we are going to heaven and enjoy a relationship with God while we live on Earth. We do this by admitting that we need a Savior, believing Jesus died for us on the cross, and receiving the Lord's forgiveness.

Girl to Girl:

Sometimes I wish I could see God face-to-face. I wish I could take a rocket ship and get to him. Getting to know him seems quite difficult. How do you get to know someone you can't even see?

Well, I have found three ways to get to know him better:

1. Receive Jesus as your Lord and Savior (Mom covered that).

2. Read the Bible to know him more.

3. Pray, pray, pray!

When I was five years old, I told my mom I wanted Jesus to be my Lord and Savior. We talked about what that meant, and I prayed a prayer to receive him as my Savior.

I pray a lot too. Sometimes God answers in the ways I hope for, and sometimes he doesn't, but I keep talking to him. (We'll talk more about unanswered prayers later in this book!)

Our family reads the Bible together too. Reading the Bible helps us understand who God is.

There are many ways to get to know God better, but the first step is to receive Jesus as your Savior. Have you done that yet? If not, keep reading, and we will show you how!

Talk About It:

- Have you received the gift Jesus offered when he took the punishment for your sins on the cross? If so, when did this gospel message first make sense to you in your mind? If not, what is stopping you from receiving Jesus' gift?

- Do you believe Jesus is the only way to know God? How does the Bible affirm or oppose your belief?

Pray Together:

The following prayer is a good prayer to receive Jesus as your Savior for the first time. It is also a good prayer if you already know Jesus as your Savior:

Jesus, thank you for dying on the cross and receiving the punishment for my sins. I recognize that I have sinned and deserve punishment. I receive your forgiveness, believe you died for me, and want to follow you all of my life. Come into my life and lead me. Amen.

Journal Later:

When you think about God, what comes to mind? Describe what you know about him based on your life experiences and what you have learned by reading the Bible.

Mom's Reflection:

_____

_____

_____

_____

_____

_____

_____

_____

_____

_____

_____

_____

Daughter's Reflection:

_____

_____

_____

_____

_____

_____

_____

_____

_____

_____

_____

_____

_____

_____

_____

_____

Close to Jesus

Now this is eternal life: that they know you, the only true God, and Jesus Christ, whom you have sent.

John 17:3

Mom's Thoughts:

Summertime has always been my favorite season. When I was a girl, I loved summer because I enjoyed the break from school. I also loved summer because my dad was a teacher and was home more often in the summer months.

I was a tomboy, and I wanted to be just like my dad. It didn't matter if he was running his beagles, trimming the Christmas trees behind the house, building dams in the creek, fishing, or jogging. I wanted to be wherever my dad was.

Spending long summer days with my dad helped us establish a strong relationship. I wanted to know everything about him, and I wanted to follow in his footsteps. In the same way, God wants us to crave a close relationship with him. He wants us to talk to him all day long, enjoy his presence, and let him teach us.

Today's verse tells us that eternal life is more than life after death in heaven. Eternal life begins the moment we receive Jesus as Lord. Jesus wants us to spend time with him—similar to how I spent summer days with my dad—as we get to know him more deeply.

Jesus wants you to learn to talk to him throughout your days and get to know him more deeply as you face both joyful and difficult times. Walking with him while you live on Earth will change your life.

Girl to Girl:

As my mom said, eternal life is happening here on Earth! And here on Earth, God also loves to hear from you. Talking to him helps you develop a stronger and closer relationship with him.

A few years ago, I saved a moth from drowning and brought it home. I took it to the porch, held it in my hand, and tried to get it to fly away. When it didn't fly, I closed my eyes and prayed a prayer that went something like this: *"Dear Lord, I took time to save this cute, tiny moth, and I wish for it to be happy and free. Please, Lord, tell it to fly away to live the rest of its life. Amen."*

The moment I opened my eyes, the moth flew away. Moments like these help me feel close to the Lord.

God wants to talk with you too. He wants to know you, so don't be afraid to talk to him. The more you talk to God, the closer your relationship with him will become. And as my mom shared, your eternal life is happening now. Talking to God is a simple way to grow in your relationship with him.

Talk About It:

- How often do you think about Jesus throughout the average day? What could you do to remind yourself to talk to him more often?

- What one step can you take today to draw closer to Jesus and grow in your relationship with him? Brainstorm together and try to come up with a list of ideas. We'll explore creative ways to recharge with Jesus in our next devotion!

Pray Together:

Jesus, thank you for calling us into a relationship with you from the moment we receive you as Savior. Sometimes, it's hard to know how to connect with you. We ask you to open our hearts and minds to connect with you more often and in creative ways. Amen.

Journal Later:

Describe a time when you talked to God and deeply sensed that he heard you. If this has never happened to you, share a memory from a time when God cared for you by providing for you in some way (healing a sickness, giving you a friend, helping you be brave, comforting you, or encouraging you).

Mom's Reflection:

_____

_____

_____

_____

_____

_____

_____

_____

_____

_____

_____

_____

_____

_____

_____

_____

Daughter's Reflection:

_____

_____

_____

_____

_____

_____

_____

_____

_____

_____

_____

_____

_____

How to Recharge With Jesus

Come to me, all you who are weary and burdened, and I will give you rest.

Matthew 11:28

Mom's Thoughts:

What do you do when you want to relax at the end of a long day? Do you zone out with a movie, play a video game, or read a book? Maybe you like to draw, exercise, or enjoy your pet. These can all be helpful ways to unwind.

In our previous reading, we challenged you to embrace "eternal life" in the here-and-now by getting to know Jesus more intimately. Spending time with Jesus is a wonderful way to recharge when you are tired and stressed.

There are lots of ways to spend time with Jesus. Here are a few ideas:

- Turn out the lights, relax in a comfy spot, and listen to worship music.

- Draw a picture of something that makes you feel restful while imagining Jesus is sitting with you.

- Color in a Bible verse coloring book.

- Take photos in nature and enjoy God's creation.

- Sip hot cocoa (or your favorite beverage) and read a Psalm.

- Go for a hike or a walk and imagine the breeze blowing your cares away.

- Enjoy your favorite hobby while listening to worship music and thinking about Jesus' presence with you.

Can you add any more ideas to this list? Jesus invites us to come to him in our weariness, and he promises to give us rest. It's helpful to talk about what this looks like as we aim to live it out. We encourage you to try one of these ideas together today!

Girl to Girl:

My mom taught me a helpful way to rest with Jesus, and I want to share it with you today. Are you ready? Read through these steps, and then try it for yourself:

First, close your eyes and let your body relax for a minute. Make sure you're calm and comfy.

Next, imagine you are relaxing in a peaceful, beautiful place. If nothing comes to mind, ask the Lord to help you imagine a place or think of a place you visited in the past. It might be a beach, forest, waterfall, mountaintop, or even your own bedroom.

Imagine you are there. Feel the air on your skin. Look around and enjoy the beautiful and peaceful sights. Smell the aromas in the air. Hear the sounds. Enjoy being there. Let thankfulness grow in your heart and thank Jesus for the lovely place.

The Bible says that Jesus is always with his children. Thank Jesus for being with you in your peaceful place and imagine resting with him for a few minutes.

When your time with him is finished, open your eyes, and share your experience with your mom. You just connected with Jesus in a new way, and you can do this after a tough day or anytime!

Talk About It:

- Try resting with Jesus as Bekah described above. Mom, you might want to verbally walk your daughter through this exercise to help her relax and envision her peaceful place. Afterward, talk about the way you feel after resting with Jesus for a few minutes.

- Which idea for recharging with Jesus in the list above most appeals to you? When might you find time to recharge with Jesus on a more regular basis?

Pray Together:

Lord, we thank you for your great love for us. Thank you that your love is capable of replenishing us when we feel empty. Help us remember to make it a priority to rest in your love. Amen.

Journal Later:

Describe an activity that makes you feel alive, passionate, and inspired. What might it look like to invite Jesus into this activity and enjoy it while enjoying his presence with you? (Listening to worship music, talking to Jesus, or listening to an audiobook about Jesus while enjoying the activity are all great ideas.)

Mom's Reflection:

_____

_____

_____

_____

_____

_____

_____

_____

_____

_____

_____

_____

_____

_____

_____

_____

_____

Daughter's Reflection:

_____

_____

_____

_____

_____

_____

_____

_____

_____

_____

_____

Beautifully Different

I praise you because I am fearfully and wonderfully made; your works are wonderful, I know that full well.

Psalm 139:14

Mom's Thoughts:

Have you ever felt pressure to try to be like the people surrounding you? Maybe you joined a club or a team and everyone around you seemed similar. Maybe they all had great hair or super-cute, sporty outfits. Suddenly, you felt frumpy and out of place with your ponytail and T-shirt. You watched the way the other girls talked and joked, and you felt an intense desire to be more like them and fit into the same image.

Most of us know how it feels to want to fit in—even if it means pretending to be someone we're not. It's not wrong to want to fit in with others, but God wants you to know something important today: He intentionally designed you to be one of a kind. The parts of you that make you unique are the gifts he wants you to carry into the world.

Don't try to fit the mold. Be your real self. Hold your head high. Don't take yourself too seriously. Be willing to laugh at yourself. You will carry God's love to the world when you show them the real you.

Bekah would be the first to tell you that I'm sportier and woodsier than most of her friends' moms. I love running, hiking, camping, fishing, and anything outdoors. I spent years hiding these parts of my life from others, but God finally showed me that these parts of me are the exact gifts he wants to use to help other women feel free to be themselves as well!

Girl to Girl:

I think of it this way: There are these geckos called mourning geckos, and the females don't need a male to have babies. That means that the babies are just duplicates of their mothers. Crazy, right?!

Imagine how boring the world would be if we were all exactly the same. We would all look the same, talk the same, and have the same hobbies. Even worse, you could never tell anyone apart!

You might be thinking, "Well, Bekah, what makes you unique?"

Let me tell you!

As I mentioned earlier, I have a collection of reptiles in my room, and I'm always adding to the collection (even though my mom says we will *never* have a snake in this house)!

Don't worry! You don't have to collect reptiles just to be different. Your personality is what makes you special! There is no one else exactly like you on this whole planet, and God has a purpose for you just the way you are.

You can be your true self by choosing the style of clothes you like, embracing your hobbies, and letting your true personality shine. Don't be afraid to be your fun, unique self! You never need to be someone you're not!

Talk About It:

- Describe a time when you felt pressure to fit into the crowd or change to match a certain image. How did you respond in this situation?

- Name three or four of your unique talents or traits. In what ways might God want to use your unique talents, traits, and experiences to reach others with his love?

Pray Together:

Lord Jesus, thank you for creating each of us in unique and individual ways. Help us embrace our uniqueness instead of trying to blend in and be like others. Show us how you want to use our special traits and talents to change the world. Amen.

Journal Later:

Name your most unique characteristic. Share one idea for how you could bless someone else with your unique characteristic this week. For example, you might use your artistic skills to make a gift for a loved one, cheer someone up with your sense of humor, or invite a friend to enjoy a unique hobby with you.

Mom's Reflection:

_____

_____

_____

_____

_____

_____

_____

_____

_____

_____

_____

_____

_____

_____

_____

_____

_____

Daughter's Reflection:

_____

_____

_____

_____

_____

_____

_____

_____

_____

_____

_____

_____

How to Know God's Will

Rejoice always, pray continually, give thanks in all circumstances; for this is God's will for you in Christ Jesus.

1 Thessalonians 5:16-18

Mom's Thoughts:

A few years ago, I heard a famous Christian speaker at a conference. Her message was "How to Know God's Will." I was so excited. I thought she would show me exactly how to find the perfect career and feel entirely fulfilled in my life.

I was surprised when she spent the entire afternoon speaking on 1 Thessalonians 5:16-18. She taught us that we fulfill God's will by rejoicing always, praying nonstop, and giving thanks in all circumstances.

Throughout the years since the conference, I've realized the speaker was right about God's will. Embracing these three simple teachings leads to a blessed and abundant life. Let's take a closer look at each of these three commands today.

First, we're told to rejoice always. This sounds easy, but if you've ever tried to be joyful in a tough time, you know it can be difficult. God wants us to fall so deeply in love with Jesus that his joy becomes our joy—even when life is hard.

Second, we are to pray continually. I like to think of this kind of prayer as living with a constant awareness that God is with me. His presence guides me, and I talk to him throughout the day as I would talk to a friend. We'll talk more about how to pray all day in the next devotion.

Third, we're told to give thanks in all circumstances. When we believe that God works everything for good in our lives, we can find reasons to give thanks even when life is difficult.

Looking back, I realize that the famous speaker was right. A joyful, prayerful, thankful heart is always God's will.

Girl to Girl:

A few months ago, my dad and my brother Caleb were planning a trip to visit my grandparents. My grandparents live four hours away, and it was going to be a long trip. Dad let us decide whether to stay home with Mom and our youngest brother Aiden or join him on the trip. I feared it was going to be boring and thought I might have more fun at home. But I also wanted to see my grandparents. I didn't know what to do!

I asked God to show me what to do, but I didn't get a clear answer. I ultimately decided to visit my grandparents, and I'm glad I did! Through the experience, I learned that God doesn't always give us clear answers for making specific decisions; instead, he gives us the freedom to make the best decisions we can make. God is more focused on our attitudes. He wants us to be joyful, prayerful, and thankful. These attitudes are always his will for us!

Talk About It:

- Have you ever asked God to show you what he wanted you to do in a certain circumstance? Did he show you what to do?

- Today's verse shows us that God is most concerned about our hearts. He wants us to be joyful, prayerful, and thankful at all times. When we follow him in these three ways, he often gives us freedom in our decision-making. Which one of today's three commands can you deliberately focus on this week as you aim to live in God's will?

Pray Together:

Lord Jesus, we want to be joyful, prayerful, and thankful. Help us honor you with the attitudes of our hearts as we seek to live in accordance with your will at all times. We ask you to fill us with your joy, help us consider you throughout our days in prayer, and remind us to give thanks in all circumstances. Amen.

Journal Later:

Name five things that are bringing you joy in life right now. Spend a few minutes thinking about how much you appreciate these gifts. How do you feel after savoring God's gifts for a few minutes?

Mom's Reflection:

_____

_____

_____

_____

_____

_____

_____

_____

_____

_____

_____

_____

_____

_____

_____

_____

Daughter's Reflection:

_____

_____

_____

_____

_____

_____

_____

_____

_____

_____

_____

_____

_____

Praying All Day

And pray in the Spirit on all occasions with all kinds of prayers and requests.

Ephesians 6:18

Mom's Thoughts:

Have you ever been infatuated? Infatuation isn't a common word, but it means you're extremely passionate about something. You might be infatuated with a new tech gadget, video game, hobby, or even a boy! When you're infatuated, you can't get the object of your infatuation out of your mind.

Let's imagine you're infatuated with the boy who sits beside you in science class. He has shaggy blonde hair, the bluest eyes you've ever seen, and an adorable smile.

You often catch yourself thinking about Science Class Boy throughout the day. You imagine what it would be like to show him around your house, eat lunch together, and talk about your favorite TV show. Even when you're not consciously focusing on him, he's never far from your thoughts.

Praying continually is kind of like thinking about your crush throughout the day. Instead of thinking about your crush, you think about Jesus. You think about him while you do your chores, walk through the hallways at school, and hang out with friends. He's never far from your mind. And here's the best news: Unlike your crush, Jesus has promised that his presence *is* with us throughout every moment of every day!

One dimension of praying nonstop is simply staying aware of Jesus' presence with you throughout your days. You immediately remember to ask him for help when you face troubling situations. You thank him for gifts like smiles from friends, sunny days, ice cream, and laughter. You imagine him smiling at you, and you find comfort in knowing he is with you.

Unlike infatuated thoughts toward a crush, you don't romantically think about Jesus; instead, you talk to him like a trusted friend. You know he always wants what's best for you, and he's always eager to listen to you. This is how you pray nonstop!

Girl to Girl:

You might think you're doing everything you need to do to stay close to Jesus. You go to church, read books like this devotional, and pray at least once a day. These are important ways to seek Jesus, but it's easy to forget about him throughout your days. Jesus loves you so much that he wants to talk to you *all day long*!

Here's what praying all day long might look like: Before taking a test, you say a short prayer thanking Jesus for the knowledge he gives you. Later, you ask him how to encourage a friend who is having a bad day. Throughout the day, you ask him for wisdom for important decisions. There are many ways to talk to Jesus throughout the day.

You might be thinking, "Bekah, how do I remember?"

My answer is simple: Be creative! You could do what my mom did for a while and wear a different ring or bracelet to remind you to stop and talk to Jesus. It's up to you! Just remember that the Lord loves you and always wants to talk to you.

Talk About It:

- Have you ever been infatuated with something (or someone)? How often did you think about the object (or person)? What is God showing you about focusing on Jesus with this same kind of passion?

- What steps could you take to remind yourself to think of Jesus and talk to him more often throughout your days?

Pray Together:

Jesus, thank you for your desire to be with us all the time. Help us become more aware of your presence with us as we learn to enjoy you throughout our everyday moments more often. Amen.

Journal Later:

Analyze your thoughts throughout the past 24 hours. What did you think about more than anything else—a friend, a new app, a hobby, or a difficult situation? Jesus wants our thoughts to return to him often throughout our days. What is God showing you about your thoughts?

Mom's Reflection:

_____

_____

_____

_____

_____

_____

_____

_____

_____

_____

_____

_____

_____

_____

_____

_____

Daughter's Reflection:

_____

_____

_____

_____

_____

_____

_____

_____

_____

_____

_____

_____

Don't Buy the Lie

For our struggle is not against flesh and blood, but against the rulers, against the authorities, against the powers of this dark world and against the spiritual forces of evil in the heavenly realms.

Ephesians 6:12

Mom's Thoughts:

When you think about Satan, you might imagine a fiery figure with horns and a pitchfork. Satan is evil, but he usually doesn't show up looking like a fiery monster. Instead, he attacks us through fearful thoughts and clever lies. He often tries to throw us off course in ways that are almost too subtle to notice.

Here are a few examples of "random" thoughts that are actually attacks from Satan:

- "I'm so dumb. Why do I always say such stupid things?"

- "I'll never fit in here."

- "I'll never be good enough."

- "No one likes me."

- "There's nothing special about me."

We all face these thoughts at times. Most people assume these are just insecurities bubbling up from somewhere deep within them. In reality, these thoughts are attacks from Satan himself. If he can convince us to think terrible things about ourselves, he knows he can stop us from fulfilling our God-given purposes on Earth.

Are you believing any of the devil's lies when you think about yourself? The Apostle Paul tells us how to protect ourselves from the enemy's attacks: When Satan speaks lies, we speak back with the Word of God.

Satan tempted Jesus when he walked on Earth, and Jesus responded by speaking God's Word to the devil. Three times, Satan tempted Jesus in the desert, and each of these three times, Jesus responded by quoting a Bible verse. Jesus' weapon was the Word, and he has given us this weapon to overcome the devil as well!

I've learned to follow Jesus' example and respond to untrue thoughts with the Word of God. I've also learned that reading, memorizing, and studying the Bible helps me recognize Satan's attacks more quickly. When you recognize Satan's lies, speak God's Word. You will overcome the enemy's attack.

Girl to Girl:

Last year in school, I didn't get many of my close friends in my class. One time at the beginning of the year, the teacher told us to partner up, and it looked like no one picked me.

A thought went through my head that went something like, "No one likes you."

That's when I silently talked back to the thought and said, "No, stop!"

I decided I wasn't going to believe the lie that no one likes me. Instead, I went over to an old friend, offered to be her partner, and now we're closer than ever. The situation reminded me that difficult and insecure moments can actually help us develop new and deeper friendships. These moments also help us remember not to believe Satan's mean thoughts. We can take a stand against untrue thoughts!

Talk About It:

- Sit quietly for a moment and ask God to show you a lie you have believed about yourself. Share anything that comes to mind.

- What biblical truth could you memorize to help you stand against this lie in the future? If nothing comes to mind, search for a verse right now, write it down, and work on memorizing it.

- Why do you think the devil attacks us in sneaky ways instead of showing up with fiery horns and a pitchfork like we see in the movies?

Pray Together:

Lord Jesus, thank you that you defeated Satan when you died on the cross. We claim your authority as we stand on your truth and cast out the lies we have believed. Thank you for reigning over evil and being all-powerful in our lives. Amen.

Journal Later:

What untrue thought have you believed about yourself in the past or present? What is God showing you about this thought?

Mom's Reflection:

_____

_____

_____

_____

_____

_____

_____

_____

_____

_____

_____

Daughter's Reflection:

_____

_____

_____

_____

_____

_____

_____

_____

_____

_____

_____

_____

_____

Listen Up!

To answer before listening—that is folly and shame.

Proverbs 18:13

Mom's Thoughts:

When I was younger, I had a friend who tried to "outdo me" almost every time I told her a story from my life. Often, I could tell she was thinking about what she wanted to say instead of listening to me. She often interrupted me, and she didn't seem to care about anything I tried to share with her.

One time, I told her that our dog had just given birth to five puppies. She interrupted to tell me about a time when her dog had nine puppies.

Another time, I told her that our family went to a little cabin in the woods for summer vacation. Instead of asking about our trip, she told me that her family went to an enormous log cabin for summer vacation. She always wanted to have the biggest, best, most fabulous stories, and she was not a good listener.

Listening well is one of the best ways to show someone you care about them. Think about it—do you feel valued when a friend constantly interrupts you, directs every conversation back to herself, or tries to outdo you when sharing stories? Probably not.

Let's look at a few characteristics of good listeners:

- Good listeners are thoughtful and engaged. They maintain eye contact and express compassion using kind words and facial expressions.

- They ask follow-up questions.

- They don't turn every conversation back to themselves.

- They are fully engaged and not distracted by their phones or anything else.

You will carry God's love into your relationships by learning to listen well. People will want to spend time with you because everyone needs a place where they will be heard and loved. Be a good listener. You will soon find that your life is overflowing with friends.

Girl to Girl:

I can relate to what my mom wrote. There's a girl in my school who always tries to show how amazing she is by telling big stories about her life. When I try to talk to her, she often interrupts me and never seems to pay attention to what I'm saying. It's frustrating and sort of makes me want to scream!

I've learned that the best thing to do in these situations is just to listen. Being patient with frustrating people isn't usually easy, but it's helpful to remember that God is patient with us. I remind myself that God listens to me every day and is always patient with me.

Being a good listener can help us make friends, and it's a great way to show the love of God. Think about it, when someone listens to you and asks good questions, you know they care about you, and that's one of the best feelings in the world!

Talk About It:

- Do you know anyone who frequently interrupts you when you try to talk? How does this make you feel?

- Name someone in your life who is a good listener. What makes this person easy to talk to? How do you feel when you are with this person?

Pray Together:

Lord, you have called us to love our neighbors as ourselves, and this kind of love includes listening to others the way we want them to listen to us. Help us focus on the needs in front of us when other people are speaking. We want to be caring and compassionate listeners. Amen.

Journal Later:

Would you describe yourself as a good listener? We discussed several characteristics of good listeners in the list above. Which one of these traits could you work on as you listen to others this week?

Mom's Reflection:

_____

_____

_____

_____

_____

_____

_____

_____

_____

_____

_____

_____

_____

_____

_____

_____

Daughter's Reflection:

_____

_____

_____

_____

_____

_____

_____

_____

_____

_____

_____

Excellence Instead of Perfection

And whatever you do, whether in word or deed, do it all in the name of the Lord Jesus, giving thanks to God the Father through him.

Colossians 3:17

Mom's Thoughts:

I was in middle school when I set out on a quest to be perfect. I couldn't stand getting anything less than an A on every test, and I wanted to be the best artist, the fastest runner, and the best writer in my class. Looking back now, I see that my desire for perfection was partially about doing my best, but it was also about pride.

You may or may not be holding yourself to a standard of perfection at school, but I imagine there's some area of your life in which you'd like to be perfect. You want to be the perfect friend, the perfect musician, or the perfect Christian. Maybe you always want your outfits to be perfect, or you're all about having the perfect hair.

Your pursuit of perfection might work for a few years. You might do well in school, have lots of popular friends, and get good grades. However, sooner or later, you're going to make a mistake, fail to achieve perfection, and feel like you've failed.

Throughout the past few years, I've learned a simple phrase that has released me from my exhausting pursuit of perfection: "Pursue excellence, not perfection." This simple phrase sets me free by reminding me that it's okay to make mistakes. I don't have to be perfect. I just need to give my best.

Perfection is an unattainable goal because only God is perfect. If the pursuit of perfection has you stressed out and feeling defeated, change your motto. Stop striving for perfection and strive for excellence instead.

Girl to Girl:

"AHHHHH! I GOT A C!!!!! It's the worst thing that's ever happened to me on the face of this Earth!"

Have you ever felt like this? Maybe you studied for hours, and someone who didn't study at all got a better grade. It stinks.

It feels good to get good grades and be the best at things that are important to us, but guess what? God cares about one thing even more: He cares that you tried your best.

My mom tells me she doesn't care if I don't always get A's. She just wants me to try my best and then not stress out over the results.

I've learned that it's better to give my best effort than to get 110 percent!

My mom and I aren't telling you to slack off and quit studying. We just want to encourage you to give your very best and then try not to stress out over the results! Perfection is way overrated.

Talk About It:

- In what area of your life is God calling you to exchange perfectionism for excellence?

- What would it look like for you to stop trying to be perfect in this area, let go of your desire for control, and pursue excellence instead? (Be specific: What grades would be acceptable? What sort of performance would be excellent without needing to be perfect?)

- How does the pursuit of excellence set us free from the unattainable goal of achieving perfection?

Pray Together:

God, we know that only you are perfect. Thank you for being holy and calling us to follow you in holiness. As we pursue you, help us set aside our prideful desires for perfection and find peace in knowing that we are giving our best efforts and leaving the outcomes in your hands. Amen.

Journal Later:

Do you put pressure on yourself to be perfect in any area of your life? How does this pressure make you feel? What is one thing your family could do to help you pursue excellence instead of perfection? For example, would you like your parents to put less pressure on you when it comes to your grades or after-school activities?

Mom's Reflection:

_____

_____

_____

_____

_____

_____

_____

_____

_____

_____

_____

_____

_____

_____

_____

_____

Daughter's Reflection:

_____

_____

_____

_____

_____

_____

_____

_____

_____

_____

_____

_____

Big Worries

Therefore I tell you, do not worry about your life.

Matthew 6:25

Mom's Thoughts:

Do you feel stressed out about anything today? You might be stressed about a project due at school, a big test, a friendship, or something hard happening within your family. Maybe you're worried about whether you're going to make it into the school musical or make it onto a team. At times, it probably feels like your mind is consumed by your stressful situation.

We all face worries and stressful situations, but we don't have to be consumed by these situations. I've learned that most of what causes me daily stress isn't big enough to make it into the book of my life.

Here's what I mean: If I ever write a book about my life, I probably won't mention the stress I felt when I had to get braces or the test I failed in seventh-grade social studies (both true stories!). I won't write about the time my older sister's car broke down on the way to school or the boy who broke my heart in eighth grade. These events are simply not in the book!

Whatever you're facing feels huge today. You might have lost a loved one or faced a devastating loss. These events *will* make it into the book of your life. But when it comes to the small stressors of your daily life, take a deep breath, calm your nerves, and remind yourself of these words: "Girl, this won't even make it into the book."

Girl to Girl:

Stress—I sure don't like stress at all! Stress is a feeling of overwhelming nervousness, and it can do real damage to your mind if you have too much.

As you know, I own many reptiles. I have fun with them, but sometimes, I feel stressed about them. One time, my gecko was trying to shed, and I needed to get the skin off of its toes. My turtle tank also needed an upgrade! I was totally overwhelmed with stress.

My dad said, "Bekah, your brain is going a million miles an hour right now. I need you to calm down and breathe."

I took a deep breath, and then we talked it through. It helped a lot.

Another tip my guidance counselor taught me is to do something called "square breathing." You imagine drawing a vertical line in the air while breathing in. Next, you hold your breath while drawing the top horizontal line. You exhale while drawing the other vertical line downward, and you finish the bottom horizontal line of the square by resting.

My mom shared that small things sometimes feel huge, and I completely agree with her! I joined the band at school last year, and I couldn't keep up with practicing. I was sooo stressed! Another time, I forgot to do my homework, realized it at 10:00 p.m., and it was super stressful. These things happen to us all. When you feel stressed, take a deep breath and remind yourself that what feels huge today probably won't feel huge in a month. Most likely, it won't even make it into the book!

Talk About It:

- What is causing you the most stress in your life right now?

- If you were to write a book about your life one day, would this stressor make it into the book? How does this realization help you keep today's stress in perspective?

Pray Together:

God, we thank you for caring about us so deeply. Help us give you our worries and turn our stress over to you as we remember that many of the things that cause us stress will be forgotten in a few weeks, months, or years. Amen.

Journal Later:

Describe a time in the past when you were stressed, but now you can look back on it and laugh about it.

Mom's Reflection:

_____

_____

_____

_____

_____

_____

_____

_____

_____

_____

_____

_____

_____

_____

_____

Daughter's Reflection:

_____

_____

_____

_____

_____

_____

_____

_____

_____

_____

_____

Dreaming Big

He brought me out into a spacious place; he rescued me because he delighted in me.

2 Samuel 22:20

Mom's Thoughts:

Do you have any big dreams for your life? Maybe you want to be a part of the school musical, run for class president, make it onto the cheerleading squad, or be an all-star on a sports team.

When I was a teenager, one of my greatest dreams was to win a medal at the state track meet. My race was the 800-meter run, and I had visions of standing on the podium to receive my hard-earned gold medal.

Sadly, due to an injury, my dream never came to life. I'll never forget sobbing behind the bleachers at the district track meet after failing to reach my goal. I felt like a little girl standing in a dark room—alone, frustrated, and embarrassed that I had the boldness to chase a dream in the first place.

Looking back on my dream of track stardom, I'm thankful God didn't let me win a medal at the state track meet. God used my disappointment to teach me to find my identity in his love instead of finding my identity through my abilities. He taught me that some dreams fall apart because he is protecting us, and his ways are always better than our ways.

Keep dreaming big and keep chasing your dreams. But don't forget to ask God to help you follow him as you set goals and strive to reach them. And when your dreams don't work out according to your hopes, remind yourself that God is protecting you. He has something even better in store.

Girl to Girl:

Little four-year-old Bekah loved to go down to the creek. She would go with her mom and baby brother and try to catch fish, frogs, toads, newts, and anything she could get her hands on. Her mother would always say, "Let's take them home for one night, and tomorrow we'll come back and let them go."

Bekah loved creating habitats for her creatures in her small aquarium. She loved pretending she ran a "Froggy Hotel." Meanwhile, deep inside, she wanted more. She wanted a creature she could keep forever.

She often asked if she could keep the creatures, but her parents would say, "Sweetie, they will miss their friends. They need to live in the wild."

Little Bekah felt sad to let them go.

Keeping creatures as pets was a dream I tried to chase for years, but the ending was always the same—we had to let them go. But then something wonderful happened! Three years ago, I got a turtle! That was the beginning of a new phase. Before long, we added another turtle, and I've had all sorts of pets throughout the years.

It took hard work to save money and buy these pets at the pet store, but it's been worth it. Unlike the wild creatures we used to find at the creek, these creatures thrive in the habitats we have created in tanks in my bedroom!

Remember this: If a dream doesn't work out the way you wanted, God might be closing one door, but he is capable of opening another one—a better one!

Talk About It:

- What is your greatest dream right now?

- Have you ever felt disappointed because a dream didn't work out the way you expected? What was your dream, and how did it turn out? What might God want to teach you about his purpose for you regarding this dream?

Pray Together:

Lord, thank you for giving us big dreams for our lives. Help us stay close to you as we discern what it might look like to follow your lead and stay in step with you as we pursue our dreams. We want to honor you and bring you glory as we fulfill your purpose for our lives. Amen.

Journal Later:

Imagine your greatest dream becomes a reality. Describe what that would look like in your life.

Mom's Reflection:

_____

_____

_____

_____

_____

_____

_____

_____

_____

_____

_____

_____

_____

_____

_____

_____

Daughter's Reflection:

_____

_____

_____

_____

_____

_____

_____

_____

_____

_____

God's Protection

In fact, this is love for God: to keep his commands. And his commands are not burdensome.

1 John 5:3

Mom's Thoughts:

What's the first word that comes to mind when you think of the Bible? Some people think the Bible is a book of rules intended to steal their fun and make life boring. Other people think the Bible is an instruction manual for how to live a godly life.

When I was younger, I had the false belief that following God's guidelines in the Bible would take away my joy and freedom. I wanted to live by my own rules, and some of the commands in the Bible seemed unreasonable to me. Sadly, I didn't understand that every one of God's boundaries in the Bible is for our protection and well-being.

Jesus is not trying to stifle your fun, steal your joy, or force you to become someone you're not. Every command in Scripture is to protect you and help you live your very best life.

The Bible is more than a set of rules. It's a love letter from the One who loves us more than we could ever imagine. More than anything else, the Bible is about God's love for us. Woven throughout the Old and New Testaments is the most beautiful love story ever written—the story of how God loved us so much that he sent his Son to die for us.

After several years of living by my own rules, I finally turned to God and decided to live within his boundaries. The most surprising shift took place: I discovered realms of joy and freedom I never dreamed of!

Girl to Girl:

I agree with my mom on this one! God doesn't want you to live your life thinking that the Bible is nothing but restrictions. The Bible is a story. It's a story of how to follow God and serve him. It's a story about brave people who served him. Most of all, it's a story about how much he has loved us since before the beginning of time.

The Bible does include instructions about how to live, but God isn't denying us full access to enjoyable lives. He is protecting us.

You've probably heard your parents say, "Look both ways when crossing the road."

Our parents give us instructions to protect us. In the same way, God tells us how to live because he loves us more than we could ever imagine, and he wants to protect us. Here's the best news: Following God's directions won't steal your happiness. Instead, we find happiness by following God.

God is like a good dad watching his children play in the yard and making sure they don't run into the road, fall into the swimming pool, or climb the wrong tree! He wants us to live with joy and peace, and he wants to protect us.

Talk About It:

- Spend a few minutes pondering the reality that every command in the Bible is for your good, your joy, and your protection. How does this change the way you view the Bible?

- See if you can name the Ten Commandments. (Turn to Exodus 20:1-17 for help.) As you reflect on these commandments, describe how these commands might offer protection. What bad outcomes could result from disobedience?

Pray Together:

Lord God, thank you for giving us your written Word. Help us grow in our understanding of your love as we remember that every word in the Bible is for our protection. Thank you for your love letter to us. Help us fall in love with your Word. Amen.

Journal Later:

Describe a time when you were hurt by sin—your sin or someone else's. In what way would this situation have worked out differently if everyone involved had stayed within the protection of God's boundaries?

Mom's Reflection:

_____

_____

_____

_____

_____

_____

_____

_____

_____

_____

_____

_____

_____

_____

_____

_____

_____

Daughter's Reflection:

_____

_____

_____

_____

_____

_____

_____

_____

_____

_____

_____

_____

_____

Stormy Weather

He got up, rebuked the wind and said to the waves,
"Quiet! Be still!"

Mark 4:39

Mom's Thoughts:

Yesterday, we awakened to a world encased in a silver sheen of ice. Crystal droplets, frozen in time, hung from the railing of the deck like daggers waiting to fall. The wind howled, and frozen shards flew from the jostled branches of the poplar tree.

The storm raged all day, and when I came home from getting groceries in the evening, Bekah was outside attempting to feed our three pet beagles. Our beagles are hunting dogs, and they are happiest living in a well-insulated kennel in the backyard, but we don't always love trekking into the weather to care for them.

"It's really windy," Bekah proclaimed as she trudged across the icy yard with a jug of warm water.

"Do you want me to help you?" I asked.

"Yes. Thanks, Mom," she said.

Together, we braved the gusty winds and took care of our animals. I was happy to help my girl and comfort her just by being with her.

In the same way, Jesus wants us to remember that he's with us in every storm we face. Storms in life are tough times—times of illness, sadness, fear, death, worries, and suffering. You've probably lived through a few storms in your life.

Today's verse shows Jesus' power over the storms we face. With a simple command to "be still," Jesus can calm any storm. Sometimes Jesus calms our storms. Other times, he is like the parent who sticks close and helps his child endure the storm—kind of like I helped Bekah take care of our chores last night.

The next time you face a storm, remember that Jesus is right beside you. You can trust that he is close to you and that he is in control.

Girl to Girl:

A few years ago, we got a new puppy. My brother and I loved playing with her. We had so much fun laughing and chasing her around the yard.

When she was just four months old, the unimaginable happened. She got sick and passed away. It was so difficult for me. She was such a great dog, and I missed her so much. After she died, I often fell asleep with tears streaming down my face. I didn't want to let her go, and I couldn't believe she was gone.

During that time, I prayed to Jesus and asked him to heal my broken heart. It didn't happen right away, but with time, I slowly started to feel better.

Praying to Jesus can help you in hard situations too. He might not stop the storm that's happening in your life—just like he didn't bring my puppy back. But he can help you feel better. Psalm 34:18 tells us that the Lord is close to the brokenhearted. He will be close to you in your difficult times too.

Talk About It:

- Does any part of your life feel like a stormy situation right now?

- How do you feel when you think about the fact that Jesus is right beside you in this storm?

- Sometimes Jesus calms the storms around us, but sometimes he lets the storms rage and walks with us through the difficulties. Why do you think he sometimes chooses to let us walk through storms?

Pray Together:

Jesus, we don't always understand why you allow us to walk through storms, and sometimes, we have difficulty sensing your presence with us. Help us trust that you are with us, even when it's hard to tell you are there. Thank you for loving us so much that you promise never to leave us. Amen.

Journal Later:

Write about a time in your life when you faced a storm and God used it to teach you a lesson or help you grow.

Mom's Reflection:

_____

_____

_____

_____

_____

_____

_____

_____

_____

_____

Daughter's Reflection:

Fear Fighting

The weapons we fight with are not the weapons of the world.
On the contrary, they have divine power to demolish
strongholds.

2 Corinthians 10:4

Mom's Thoughts:

What are you afraid of today? You might be afraid you won't get invited to a friend's birthday party, fearful you're going to fail next week's math test, or worried about messing up on a project that's important to you. Maybe a loved one is battling a terminal diagnosis, or perhaps you're afraid you're going to get in trouble at school.

We all face fears, and if we don't have tools to help us process fear with Jesus, we will be controlled by fear. A few years ago, Bekah's baby brother Aiden faced a life-threatening diagnosis. I'd never been more afraid. The thought of losing our precious baby made me feel paralyzed by fear.

After a few weeks of battling fear, a friend offered these words: "You'll defeat this fear when fear becomes a prompt that sends you running to the arms of Jesus."

My friend's words were filled with truth. Following her advice, every time I felt the familiar twinge of fear, I imagined myself running into the safe embrace of Jesus' arms.

I also discovered two simple strategies that helped me fight fear: First, I memorized a Bible verse that helped me trust God with our little boy. Every time I felt afraid, I spoke the verse out loud. Second, I picked a worship song that reminded me of God's goodness. I let the lyrics and the melody play in my head and worshiped silently in my spirit when fear felt overwhelming. It wasn't an easy battle, but fear lost its grip on me.

Let fear lead you to worship Jesus, rest in him, and stand on his Word, and it will lose its grip on you.

Girl to Girl:

We all feel afraid sometimes. When I feel afraid, the first thing I do is pray. Praying usually helps me feel better in tough situations. I know God hears my prayers, and I feel more peaceful.

My mom also writes Bible verses and hangs them on the fridge. She says we can say them when we need them. That's why she makes us remember them! A verse I repeat *a lot* reads, "When I'm afraid I will trust you" (Psalm 56:3).

Go ahead and open your Bible right now (or do an online search) and find a Bible verse about fear. Write it down and put it where you will see it. Work on memorizing it, and you will have a weapon to help you fight back every time you feel afraid.

Talk About It:

- What is the biggest fear you're facing in your life right now?

- What Bible verse can you memorize and speak when this fear arises in your heart? Take a few minutes to find a Bible verse to speak in the face of your fears.

- What worship song could you quietly sing when you face this fear in the future? If no specific song comes to mind, search online for a worship "battle song" to sing when you feel afraid.

Pray Together:

Lord, we thank you that there is no fear in your perfect love. Help us run to you when we feel afraid. Help us run to you by speaking your Word and worshiping you. Thank you that when we take our eyes off of our fears and fix them on you, we defeat the enemy with his own weapon. We take the fear that was intended to destroy us, and we use it to defeat the enemy!

Journal Later:

Describe a time in the past when you felt afraid, and God provided for you and delivered you. How does this memory help you find the courage to face the future?

Mom's Reflection:

_____

_____

_____

_____

_____

_____

_____

_____

_____

_____

_____

_____

_____

_____

_____

_____

_____

Daughter's Reflection:

_____

_____

_____

_____

_____

_____

_____

_____

_____

_____

_____

_____

Apologize First

Blessed are the merciful, for they will be shown mercy.

Matthew 5:7

Mom's Thoughts:

Most of us don't enjoy apologizing after disagreements. Especially when we're sure we are right and the other person is wrong, apologizing feels like losing the argument. Nonetheless, I've learned a powerful insight for healthy relationships: Always be willing to apologize first.

Imagine you're arguing with your brother or sister about whose turn it is to wash the dishes. You're positive it's not your turn because you remember washing the spaghetti sauce off the dishes *last night*. The argument just turned into a yelling match with slammed doors. As you sulk in your room, you know that slamming the door was wrong, but the last thing you want to do is apologize.

Or maybe your scenario looks more like this: You're having a sleepover with a friend, and you're trying to plan the evening. You want to do makeovers, but she wants to play video games. The disagreement turns into an argument. You tell her that her video games are boring and pathetic. She calls you a mean name and says she wants to call her mom. After locking yourself in the bathroom to sort through your emotions, you know you should apologize and work things out.

In each of these situations, God is giving you a choice: You can continue to sulk and allow tension to build, or you can be the bigger person and apologize first. It won't be easy to humble yourself and ask for forgiveness, but it will be the first step toward healing the relationship and moving on.

Apologizing first is really about putting people ahead of our pride. Regardless of the disagreement, we show maturity when we value relationships above our pride. Learn to apologize first as often as possible, and you will be more mature than many full-grown adults. You will also be a peacemaker and unifier.

Girl to Girl:

As you know, my brother and I aren't always the most loving siblings toward one another. We bicker quite a bit because he's younger and wants to do everything I do. This causes me to lose my patience, and we often end up fighting.

Does any of this sound familiar? Arguments happen to the best of us! The point is, after a big argument, apologizing can be tough.

I sometimes try to recover from an argument with my brother by apologizing to him in my mind. You might be asking, "Is this a bad thing?" Well, apologizing in your mind might make you feel better, but it won't fix your relationship. It's important to humble ourselves and tell our loved ones we're sorry after we treat them disrespectfully. We need to directly apologize because the relationship won't be repaired until we make things right.

Apologizing first requires strength and maturity. Do you want to be strong and mature? Learn to apologize first. You will restore peace and heal relationships.

Talk About It:

- Do you find it difficult to apologize first after an argument? What does God want to show you about setting aside your pride as you approach your relationships with humility?

- Can you describe a time when someone else apologized to you and mended the relationship quickly? How did you feel after things had been made right again?

Pray Together:

Lord, we thank you for calling us to be humble. It's not easy to set aside our pride and apologize, but we know that humility is the pathway to maturity and love. Help us always remember to put other people before our pride. Amen.

Journal Later:

Describe a recent disagreement you had with a sibling, friend, or parent. What happened, and who apologized first? How might this situation have worked out differently if you had apologized immediately?

Mom's Reflection:

_____

_____

_____

_____

_____

_____

_____

_____

_____

_____

_____

_____

_____

_____

_____

Daughter's Reflection:

_____

_____

_____

_____

_____

_____

_____

_____

_____

_____

Feeling Weak?

My grace is sufficient for you, for my power is made perfect in weakness.

2 Corinthians 12:9

Mom's Thoughts:

Are you facing any overwhelming problems today? Maybe you have an especially difficult class, and you're afraid you're not going to pass it. You might be worried about a decision you need to make, a bully who has been bothering you, or a friend who seems distant.

You might have heard that God doesn't give us more than we can handle. Whoever came up with this phrase probably wasn't familiar with the words of 2 Corinthians 12:9. This powerful verse tells us that our weakness is the perfect place for God to show up and make his power known. God *does* give us more than we can handle—and then he shows up and makes his power known by working miracles.

Are you feeling weak? Perfect! Your weakness is the backdrop for God's next miracle in your life.

God is fully capable of giving you the strength to endure every challenge you are facing today. He is fully able to guide you through a difficult school year, help you make amends in a friendship, or heal your broken heart. You might not be able to conquer what is in front of you, but God is able to empower you.

Girl to Girl:

Shortly after joining the school band last year, I had a terrible week. I lost a library book, felt stressed about practicing the clarinet, and felt overwhelmed with life in general. I was like, "GOD, WHY!??"

I kinda felt like I had a whole horse to carry on my back!

Looking back now, I realize God was showing me that what seemed to be a billion-pound weight on my back was only a speck compared to him. And he was going to help me dust it off!

Everything eventually worked out with the library book and band. God also helped me work through everything that was stressing me out. I realized that God does give us more than we can handle at times. I also learned that he is capable of providing for us when these times arrive. He just wants us to turn to him and ask him for help. When we turn to God for help, he makes his power known in our weakness.

Don't be afraid of feeling weak. Most of us try to hide it when we feel weak or scared. Instead of pretending everything is fine, ask God to come in his power and work through your weaknesses. You might be surprised by what happens next!

Talk About It:

- In which area of your life do you need God to make his power known in your weakness?

- Can you think of a time in the past when God helped you in a moment when you felt weak? Describe the situation.

Pray Together:

Lord God, your ways are much higher than our ways. We often try to run from our weaknesses and hide them from the world, but you remind us that weakness is the perfect place for you to move and work. Help us embrace our weaknesses as we watch for you to work miracles in our lives. Amen.

Journal Later:

We can embrace tiredness, illness, inadequacy, and every other form of weakness because these moments are perfect situations for God to work miracles in our lives. If you could tap into God's power and know for sure that he would give you strength in one area, in which area of your life would you like God's strength to start flowing through you? (For example, would you like more patience with a sibling, more knowledge at school, better skills in friendships, or more creativity?)

Mom's Reflection:

_____

_____

_____

_____

_____

_____

_____

_____

_____

_____

_____

_____

_____

_____

_____

_____

Daughter's Reflection:

_____

_____

_____

_____

_____

_____

_____

_____

_____

_____

_____

_____

_____

_____

_____

A Good Start

But I will sing of your strength, in the morning I will sing of your love; for you are my fortress, my refuge in times of trouble.

Psalm 59:16

Mom's Thoughts:

Do you typically wake up grumpy or cheerful? You might have a morning routine that helps you get off to a good start, or you might roll out of bed and grumble your way through breakfast. Regardless of your morning temperament, one simple habit can transform your morning—and your entire day. Beginning the day by looking toward Jesus automatically helps you focus in the right place before the day begins.

You might feel guilty because you don't have time or energy to read a chapter from your Bible or spend 30 minutes in prayer every morning. What if I told you that you could direct your attention toward Jesus every morning in less than 20 seconds?

All you need to do is begin your day by looking in Jesus' direction. Before you climb out of your bed, thank Jesus for being with you and ask him to guide you throughout the day. Or you might memorize a verse and speak it to him each morning. This simple step will transform your mornings—and your life.

Every morning, I begin my day by speaking these words: "This is the day the Lord has made; I will rejoice and be glad in it" (Psalm 118:24, my translation). These words remind me that the day ahead of me is not my own. It is a gift from God, and God wants me to rejoice and be glad throughout this day. Speaking these words helps me shift from grumpiness to joyfulness, reminds me of God's goodness, and points me back to my purpose.

Girl to Girl:

Starting the morning with God might seem like a burden, but it can transform your whole day! When you start your morning with God, he can help prepare you for whatever lies ahead of you. Encountering his goodness will help you love others throughout the rest of the day as well.

There are many ways to start your day with the Lord. First, reading your Bible is a great way to start the day. You might rest with God for a moment and imagine him smiling as you enjoy your quiet time together. Praying and asking God to direct your day is another great way to start the day.

Our family reads a devotion every morning before starting the day. (It's similar to this book!) There are many free online devotionals and books to help us connect with God. Reading these books can help you start your day off right! It doesn't matter what you choose to do. What matters most is that you direct your attention toward God. Starting your day with the Lord is always the best way to begin!

Talk About It:

- What could you do to remind yourself to look toward Jesus first thing every morning? (Consider leaving a note on your dresser or by your bed.)

- Would you describe yourself as a morning person? Are you typically happy or grumpy first thing in the morning? What would make you feel happier at the start of each new day? If you're not sure, ask God for a creative idea.

Pray Together:

God, we thank you that your plans for us are good. We also thank you that your joy becomes our strength in weary moments. We want to carry your joy wherever we go. Help us create new habits to tap into your love, peace, and joy first thing every morning. We want to begin our days with you and walk with you throughout all our days. Amen.

Journal Later:

Describe the happiest morning of your life. What made it such a happy morning?

Mom's Reflection:

_____

_____

_____

_____

_____

_____

_____

_____

_____

_____

_____

_____

_____

_____

_____

_____

_____

Daughter's Reflection:

_____

_____

_____

_____

_____

_____

_____

_____

_____

_____

_____

_____

_____

_____

God's Comfort

As a mother comforts her child, so will I comfort you.

Isaiah 66:14

Mom's Thoughts:

Do you ever try to pray before bed but end up falling asleep? For years, I felt guilty because my bedtime prayers always put me to sleep. In fact, if I was having trouble sleeping, I would start praying because I knew praying would help me drift off to sleep.

After feeling guilty about falling asleep when I prayed, God showed me something I'd never considered. Bekah was a toddler at the time, and she often had trouble sleeping. I would slip into her bed and hold her until she drifted off to sleep. Watching her fall asleep in my arms wasn't a burden. It was a gift. Watching her drift peacefully to sleep filled my heart with tender love for her.

God gently showed me that this is how he feels when his children fall asleep in his arms. Since then, I've made it a habit to fall asleep with my thoughts focused on God and his loving arms around me.

God wants to hold you in his arms as you drift off to sleep each night. This is a healing, restful, peace-filled way to end each day. When you lie down to sleep tonight, imagine God holding you in his arms and smiling over you as you drift off to sleep in the comfort of his embrace.

Girl to Girl:

We all need sleep. Our bodies need time to recuperate after long days. God wants us to learn to rest in him too. How do we rest in God's arms? I'm glad you asked.

You can rest in God's arms by lying in your bed at night and reading your Bible or a devotional book. Or you can rest in his arms by lying still and knowing he is with you and he loves you.

Many babies like to be held, and they fall asleep easily when resting in the arms of a loved one. God wants us to be like little children, which means we know how to lean into him and rest in his arms.

Thinking about God before you drift off to sleep will help lift your stress and worries. Reminding yourself that he loves you and cares for you is a great way to end any day. Try it. You might be surprised by the peace you find. You might also be surprised that this helps you fall asleep on nights when you feel restless!

Talk About It:

- How often do you have trouble falling asleep at night? What do you usually do when you can't fall asleep?

- Do you ever fall asleep during times of prayer? After reading today's devotion, what is God showing you about how he feels when you fall asleep while praying?

Pray Together:

Lord, thank you for your great love for us. Thank you for being a loving Father and for your desire to hold us in your arms and give us comfort. Help us learn to find our rest, peace, and comfort in you—whether we're falling asleep in your arms at the end of a long day or enjoying our favorite hobby while thinking about your love. Amen.

Journal Later:

God is the ultimate source of comfort in our lives, but it's easy to turn to other sources for comfort. We feel tempted to turn to friendships, food, TV, social media, and even shopping. It's not wrong to find comfort in friendships or to relax in front of the TV with a bowl of ice cream, but if these habits become our ultimate sources of comfort, we will miss out on receiving God's comfort. Where do you turn for comfort at the end of a hard day? What would it look like for you to find comfort in God instead?

Mom's Reflection:

_____

_____

_____

_____

_____

_____

_____

_____

_____

_____

_____

_____

_____

_____

_____

_____

Daughter's Reflection:

_____

_____

_____

_____

_____

_____

_____

_____

_____

_____

_____

_____

_____

Happy to Be With You

The Lord your God is with you, the Mighty Warrior who saves.
He will take great delight in you; in his love he will no longer
rebuke you, but will rejoice over you with singing.

Zephaniah 3:17

Mom's Thoughts:

Not long ago, our family wandered through the woods on an unseasonably balmy winter morning. The pungent aroma of thawing earth filled us with hopes for springtime and all the possibilities that go with warmer days. We threw rocks into the muddy creek and lounged on the sandy shoreline.

"I'm happy to be here with you guys," Bekah's two-year-old brother Aiden declared as we basked in the sunshine.

We all giggled as we enjoyed our little buddy's sentiments and agreed that we were all happy to be together.

Can you think of a time when you were genuinely happy to spend time with a friend or loved one? Maybe you had a sleepover with your best friend and were thrilled to spend time with her. You might have been enjoying a girls' day out with your mom or a poolside afternoon with your neighbors.

We know how it feels to sincerely enjoy spending time with the people we love, but some of us doubt that God could feel the same joy when spending time with us. Today's verse tells us that God enjoys us so much that he rejoices over us with singing!

After our afternoon along the creek, I decided to start a new habit. Every morning while I eat my breakfast, I talk to God. I think of sweet Aiden saying, "I'm happy to be here with you guys." I remember the joy I felt in my heart when he spoke those simple words. I then look to God and say, "Good morning, Lord.

124

I'm happy to be with you." In response, I sense that the Lord is happy to be with me too.

God is always happy to be with you. We encourage you to find a time every morning (breakfast is a great time) and tell God that you're happy to be with him. It sounds simple, but this habit can shift your whole day. Tapping into God's joy will change your attitude and your life!

Girl to Girl:

Last year for my birthday, I had a sleepover with two of my friends. We watched a movie and had a spa day, and it was so much fun. In times like these, I love being me! I just love everything about my life, my friends, and my family!

Want to hear something else? God is like a friend who loves being with you! Imagine how you would feel if no one wanted to spend time with you and do fun things with you. Sometimes, you might feel like that's true, but it's not! God always enjoys being with you. He loves you just the way you are. He cherishes your moments together. God is always happy to be with you. The more we realize this is true, the greater our joy will become too!

Talk About It:

- Describe a time when you sincerely enjoyed being with someone special to you. Where were you, and what were you doing?

- How does it make you feel when you consider that God is thrilled to be with you in this same way?

- In what ways would your life be different if you remembered that God is always happy to be with you?

Pray Together:

Jesus, we thank you for wanting to spend time with us and loving us no matter what. Help us remember that you are always happy to be with us. We are amazed when we consider that you love us so much that you rejoice over us with singing. Help us carry your love and joy into the world around us! Amen.

Journal Later:

Describe a time when you felt overwhelmed with happiness as you spent time with someone special. Where were you, what were you doing, and what made your time together so special?

Mom's Reflection:

_____

_____

_____

_____

_____

_____

_____

_____

_____

_____

_____

_____

_____

_____

_____

_____

Daughter's Reflection:

_____

_____

_____

_____

_____

_____

_____

_____

_____

_____

_____

_____

_____

_____

When Your Friends Disappoint You

Now that you have purified yourselves by obeying the truth so that you have sincere love for each other, love one another deeply, from the heart.

1 Peter 1:22

Mom's Thoughts:

You can probably think of a time when you felt disappointed by a friend. Maybe you were having a terrible day, and your friend didn't seem to care. You might have asked for help with a project, and your friend was suddenly "too busy" to help you. Maybe your friends all met up for an afternoon at the park and left you at home alone.

Other times, you might feel like you're putting all the effort into a friendship, and your friend doesn't seem to reach out to you in the same ways. It's important to remember that God isn't asking us to measure the quality of our friendships by what we receive from our friends. No friend is perfect, and every friend will eventually let you down.

A helpful way to align yourself with God when a friend disappoints you is to shift from a "receiving mindset" to a "giving mindset." A receiving mindset focuses on what others can offer us in relationships; however, a giving mindset stays focused on what we can offer to others.

A receiving mindset thinks thoughts like these: *How will this friend make me feel better about myself? In what ways will this friendship benefit me? What fun activities might I get to enjoy if I spend more time with this person?*

A giving mindset thinks thoughts such as: *What can I do to make this friend feel loved and encouraged today? How can I show my friend that she is special and important? Even though my friend hurt my feelings, how can I offer her kindness and show that I care about her?*

Instead of having high expectations for our friends and feeling hurt when they don't meet our expectations (a "receiving mindset"), God calls us to focus on what we can give to the relationships in our lives.

Girl to Girl:

All friends will eventually disappoint us because no one is perfect. You've probably faced disappointments in your friendships. For example, maybe you asked your friend to stop teasing you about your new haircut, and she got angry and decided not to sit with you at lunch.

I have had many friends disappoint me, but I know it's not a reason to get mad at them. Sometimes, we tease each other and end up getting our feelings hurt. Other times, I might ask a friend to stop doing something, but she ignores me. These moments are frustrating.

I've let friends down too. Through it all, I'm learning that friends will let each other down, but it's best not to take it personally. Everyone makes mistakes, and God wants us to look for ways to bless our friends. He wants us to look for what we can give to our friends instead of focusing on what they can do for us. The next time you feel frustrated with a friend, have a giving mindset and ask God to show you how to bless this friend.

Talk About It:

- Think about your closest friends. What sorts of blessings do these friends add to your life?

- Describe a time when a friend hurt your feelings. How did you respond? What would it look like to respond with a giving mindset in the future?

Pray Together:

Jesus, thank you for demonstrating how to selflessly give our lives away to others. Your death on the cross was the ultimate act of giving. Help us go into the world with our eyes focused on what we can give to others, not what we can receive from them. Amen.

Journal Later:

What are the three most important character traits you look for in a friend? In what ways are you currently demonstrating these traits within your current friendships?

Mom's Reflection:

_____

_____

_____

_____

_____

_____

_____

_____

_____

_____

_____

_____

_____

_____

_____

_____

Daughter's Reflection:

_____

_____

_____

_____

_____

_____

_____

_____

_____

_____

_____

_____

_____

_____

Jesus in Your Suffering

And the God of all grace, who called you to his eternal glory in Christ, after you have suffered a little while, will himself restore you and make you strong, firm and steadfast.

1 Peter 5:10

Mom's Thoughts:

Suffering is no fun, but we all endure suffering in life. Sometimes suffering is physical: an annoying cold that won't go away, a broken bone, or a chronic illness that wears you down. Other times, suffering is emotional: life disappoints you, a relationship ends, or you have to say goodbye to someone you love.

Have you ever wondered what Jesus does while we are suffering? Sometimes it feels like Jesus has abandoned us when life gets hard. It feels like he's ignoring us. However, the Bible teaches us that Jesus never abandons or ignores his children (see Hebrews 13:5).

The Bible is clear about what Jesus does when we are suffering: He has compassion for us. He weeps with us, just as he wept with Mary and Martha after the death of their brother Lazarus. The Psalms tell us he collects our tears in a bottle (see Psalm 56:8). Jesus is close to us when our hearts are broken, and he saves us when we feel crushed in spirit (see Psalm 34:18). He also promises to restore us after times of suffering by making us strong, firm, and steadfast (see 1 Peter 5:10).

The next time you are suffering, remind yourself that Jesus is right beside you. He will never leave you. He is close to you when you are hurting, and he even weeps with you. He loves you more than you could ever fathom, and you can trust him to hold you through your pain.

Girl to Girl:

I have faced plenty of hard times in my life. As I write these words to you today, I'm just beginning middle school, and let me tell you, I'm not loving it! Every day, I remind myself that God is with me, and he is here to help me through this.

You will face hard times in your life too. We all do. But when we suffer, God wants us to remember that he is with us. He's not turning his back on us or leaving us to suffer alone. As my mom said, he collects our tears in a bottle and loves us more than we can imagine.

Talk About It:

- Describe an area of your life in which you are experiencing physical or emotional pain today.

- When life is difficult, do you tend to run toward Jesus, or do you feel angry and turn the other way?

- How does the image of Jesus crying with you change the way you might respond to him in times of sadness, pain, and suffering?

Pray Together:

Jesus, thank you for using suffering in life to make us look more like you. Thank you for your tender love for us. We trust you with our broken hearts. Help us keep soft hearts as we wait for you to make us strong, firm, and steadfast. Amen.

Journal Later:

Write about a time when life felt difficult or you felt alone and heartbroken. What is God showing you about these difficult times in our lives?

Mom's Reflection:

_____

_____

_____

_____

_____

_____

_____

_____

_____

_____

_____

_____

_____

_____

_____

_____

_____

Daughter's Reflection:

_____

_____

_____

_____

_____

_____

_____

_____

_____

_____

_____

_____

_____

_____

_____

_____

_____

When No One's Watching

Whoever walks in integrity walks securely, but whoever takes crooked paths will be found out.

Proverbs 10:9

Mom's Thoughts:

Imagine everyone you know is gathered around a giant screen. The screen is about to show every moment from your past week—the public moments as well as the private moments. How much money would you pay to cancel the show?

Most of us are good at doing the right things when others are watching, but it's not always easy to do the right thing when no one is looking.

You might do a fantastic job with your household chores when your parents are watching. However, when they're not looking, you sweep dirt under doormats, shove laundry into the drawers without folding it, and hastily load the dishwasher instead of organizing it the way your parents taught you.

When no one is watching, it can be tempting to give less than your best on your homework or even cheat on a test. Maybe you watch a show you know you're not supposed to watch when your parents aren't in the room or follow a mischievous friend into trouble when you're unsupervised at a sleepover.

Integrity is doing the right thing when no one's watching. We all face times when it's tempting to slip up in the area of integrity. However, God calls us to live with integrity and do the right thing even when no one is watching.

Eating a few pieces of your little brother's Easter candy might not feel like a big deal. Swiping a loose dollar bill off the kitchen countertop might not seem like a terrible thing to do. Copying your friend's math homework might save you a few minutes. However, never forget that every decision you make—no matter how small—moves you in the direction of the woman you are becoming.

Girl to Girl:

Imagine your mom asking you to clean your room. She then goes outside to mow the lawn, and you know she'll be out there for at least two hours. No one else in your family is home. Knowing your mom will be busy outside for a while, you decide to play video games instead of cleaning your room.

This scenario could end in a variety of ways: You might clean your room after just a few minutes of video games; you might totally forget to clean your room; or you might wait an hour to clean your room, putting yourself in the habit of putting off your chores instead of doing them right away.

It's important to remember that if we don't act the same when we're alone as we would act when others are watching, we build bad habits. Plus, God is always watching us, which means we should always remember that someone important *is* watching!

Talk About It:

- Reflect on the past week. Would you be embarrassed by any of your hidden behavior if someone were to find out about it?

- Did you relate to any of the examples of stretching the limits in today's devotion? Why is it important to do the right thing when no one is watching—even when it comes to small things?

Pray Together:

God, it's not always easy to do the right thing when no one is watching. We want to be women of integrity, but we need your Spirit to guide us and help us. We ask you to convict us when we go astray and guide us so that our actions always honor you—especially when no one seems to be watching. Amen.

Journal Later:

Describe a time when you did not act with integrity in a hidden moment. Did you get caught? How did you feel about it afterward? What did God teach you through the experience?

Mom's Reflection:

_____

_____

_____

_____

_____

_____

_____

_____

_____

_____

_____

_____

_____

_____

_____

_____

Daughter's Reflection:

_____

_____

_____

_____

_____

_____

_____

_____

_____

_____

_____

_____

_____

_____

Let Your Guard Down

To the weak I became weak, to win the weak. I have become all things to all people so that by all possible means I might save some.

1 Corinthians 9:22

Mom's Thoughts:

When I was in elementary school, I cried often and easily. It didn't take long to realize my tears gave other kids a reason to make fun of me, and I learned to hide my sensitivity and turn off my tears. I spent the next 15 years trying to be strong all the time—at all costs.

Finally, near the end of my teenage years, I learned an important lesson: Appearing strong all the time makes other people feel like they can't feel weak or broken either. Some of the most powerful people—the people who are making the biggest impact on the world around them—are people who know how to share their weaknesses at appropriate times.

Think about it: Do you feel comfortable opening up to someone who seems to be strong and perfect all the time? Isn't it easier to share your problems with people who seem like they probably understand how it feels to go through similar pain?

God wants to use you to bring hope and healing to a broken world. He wants you to point others to his truth and love. Broken people don't want to open their hearts to perfect people; they prefer to share their troubles with other broken people.

You don't have to appear strong and put-together all the time. God will show you when sharing your weaknesses with others is safe. He wants you to be courageous enough to be real. When you're vulnerable with others, they will realize they don't have to be perfect either.

Girl to Girl:

Picture this: You wake up to find out your dog died. Then you realize your parents are both at work and cannot help you deal with the terrible situation. You also realize that you missed the bus while trying to make breakfast.

You're stuck walking to school in tears and are afraid the bigger kids will laugh at you. You wipe your eyes, put a serious expression on your face, and get to school. Outside your school, you see a boy sitting sadly on a bench. You walk past him wearing your most serious face. Just then, the boy wipes his eyes, gets up, and follows you into the school.

Want to know a secret? Showing our emotions helps the people around us see us as genuine people who are safe to open up to.

Think about the sad boy on the bench. If you'd let him see your sadness, you might have encouraged each other. People everywhere need encouragement, and when we're honest about our weaknesses, they will trust us enough to be honest about their troubles too.

Talk About It:

- Do you ever hide your emotions because you don't want other people to make fun of you?

- Sometimes, it's healthy to keep our emotions under control. At other times, God wants us to open our hearts and share our weaknesses with others. Name a time when it would be best to save your emotional release for a different situation. Can you think of a time when you might help someone by being honest about your weaknesses?

Pray Together:

Lord, we thank you for comforting us in our struggles so that we can comfort others. Please help us share our weaknesses at appropriate times and encourage the people you place in our lives. Thank you that your power is made perfect in our weakest moments. Amen.

Journal Later:

What is one area in which you feel weak? In what ways might God want to use this weakness to help others?

Mom's Reflection:

_____

_____

_____

_____

_____

_____

_____

_____

_____

_____

_____

_____

_____

_____

_____

_____

Daughter's Reflection:

_____

_____

_____

_____

_____

_____

_____

_____

_____

_____

_____

_____

_____

_____

Live Your Truth?

In fact, this is love for God: to keep his commands. And his commands are not burdensome.

1 John 5:3

Mom's Reflection:

Have you heard the phrase, "Live your truth"? This phrase teaches that we can each decide what is true for us, set our own rules for living, and live however we please. Sounds great, right? Well, sadly, there's a destructive lie beneath these words.

"Live your truth" implies that truth is flexible—not something that is fixed by a higher power. Contrary to the phrase "Live your truth," Jesus tells us that God's Word is Truth (see John 17:17).

Earlier in this devotional, we learned that God's commands in the Bible are for our good and our protection. When we pick and choose which parts of the Bible we will follow, we're stepping outside the umbrella of God's protection. Living by our own truths will never lead to the freedom we crave. We find freedom and joy by making God's Truth our own truth!

You're entering a time in your life when your friends will soon start "living their truths." You'll be challenged to align yourself with worldly perspectives when it comes to dating, identity, purity, the way you treat your body, and more. You'll probably be tempted to "live your truth."

Now is the time to decide what you believe about God's Word. Bekah and I encourage you to read your Bible, talk about it with trusted adults, and make up your mind to live by God's Truth—not your truth. Ultimately, God's Truth is the path to the life you crave. All other paths eventually lead to disappointment and heartache.

Girl to Girl:

Imagine you're shopping with a good friend at the mall. Your friend asks if she can head over to her favorite clothing store. You say, "Only if I can come!"

After buying cake pops and a new shirt, you only have $2.00 left in your purse as you head into the store. You're disappointed when you spot a BFF necklace for $10.00.

"Do you have any cash left over?" you ask your friend.

"I'm out of money too," your friend replies. "Why don't you just steal the necklace? It's only ten bucks, and it's small. I'm sure no one will notice."

What would you do?

Steal the necklace for your friend?

The Bible tells us not to steal. Swiping something from a store might seem like bending a small rule, but it is much more. It is disobeying the Lord and risking legal trouble. If you get caught, you'll face a fine and feel embarrassed. Even if you don't get caught, you'll probably feel guilty every time you look at the necklace, and it will feel like a barrier between you and God.

We can choose to live by our own "truths," or we can choose to live by God's Truth. God's Truth is always the pathway to peace in life.

Talk About It:

- We shouldn't expect people who aren't Christ-followers to live within the Bible's boundaries. These people need our love and not our condemnation. However, we each get to choose the truth we will follow. Do you believe everything in the Bible is true, or do you wrestle with some of the Bible's teachings?

- As you get older, you'll encounter many people who don't live in line with the Bible's teaching. They will tell you that their behavior isn't a problem because it isn't hurting anyone. Can you think of an example of one of these behaviors? (Mom, this might be a good time to initiate a conversation about the many difficult topics your daughter will soon be facing, including drugs, alcohol, and the battle for purity.)

Pray Together:

God, we thank you for giving us your Word as a source of Truth. Help us anchor ourselves in the truth of your Word so that we can stand against the deception surrounding us in the world. Amen.

Journal Later:

Imagine your friend tells you she's been stealing money from her dad. She says he has lots of money, and it's not hurting anything to steal from him. What would you say to her?

Mom's Reflection:

_____

_____

_____

_____

_____

_____

_____

_____

_____

_____

_____

Daughter's Reflection:

_____

_____

_____

_____

_____

_____

_____

_____

_____

_____

_____

_____

_____

_____

Us and Them

Love your neighbor as yourself.

Matthew 22:39

Mom's Thoughts:

I played volleyball in high school, and there was an ongoing rivalry between the volleyball players and the cheerleaders. The volleyball players often made snide remarks about the cheerleaders' outfits and peppy cheers, and the cheerleaders rolled their eyes and cracked jokes about the sweaty, muscular volleyball players.

Looking back, it seems ridiculous that we couldn't embrace our differences and get along. Sadly, the same "us and them" mentality that led to the division between the cheerleaders and the volleyball players plays itself out in destructive ways in many realms of life.

Our world would be drastically different if we all learned to set aside the "us and them" mindset. The next time you feel yourself judging someone who is different from you, remind yourself that we are all much more alike than we are different.

Some Christians subconsciously adopt an "us and them" mindset toward those who have not received Jesus as Savior. It's important to remember that even people who have not received Jesus as Savior are on a journey with God. They are either moving closer toward a life-changing encounter with Jesus or moving away from him. Rejecting people who don't know God won't lead them to an encounter with him. Instead of rejecting these people, God wants us to share his love and compassion with them.

Jesus is calling us to make disciples, and disciple-making begins when we realize we are all in the same boat. We're all in need of a Savior, and Jesus is the answer for every person. Instead of focusing on our differences, imagine the work God might do if we learned to set aside the "us and them" mentality and, instead, set out to help others move closer toward Jesus.

Girl to Girl:

God loves everyone. He also wants us to be loving toward each other. He's not talking about a mushy, romantic kind of love; instead, he wants us to love one another by showing kindness.

What does this kind of love look like? Well, maybe there's someone in your school who no one really likes or talks to. You could share God's love and kindness by befriending that person.

Some kids don't want to reach out to others who are different because they're afraid people will think they're weird. I understand, but it's important to remember that leaders aren't afraid of being different from the crowd.

Be a leader and be kind to the kids who are often rejected by others. Try to spend your time with different people and include those who often seem left out. Aim to be kind to everyone. Your true friends will understand, and you'll make an impact on everyone who notices your kindness—even those who don't know how to respond.

Talk About It:

- Are there any kids at school or in your community who feel like "them" to you? What is God showing you about these kids?

- We are all on a journey with God, and your role is to help others move toward God. How does this mindset help you move away from an "us and them" mentality?

Pray Together:

Father, help us love all of your children as you love them. We pray for tender hearts and ask you to fill us with your love in such a way that others are drawn closer to you through us. Amen.

Journal Later:

Right now, ask God to show you the face of someone in your life who is different from you—someone who feels like "them" and not "us." Ask God to shift the way you see this person and help you to see this person as "us." Write about one way you could reach out to this person in a gesture of kindness this week.

Mom's Reflection:

_____

_____

_____

_____

_____

_____

_____

_____

_____

_____

_____

_____

_____

_____

_____

_____

Daughter's Reflection:

_____

_____

_____

_____

_____

_____

_____

_____

_____

_____

_____

_____

_____

_____

_____

_____

Brokenhearted

The Lord is close to the brokenhearted and saves those who are crushed in spirit.

Psalm 34:18

Mom's Thoughts:

Where do you turn when you feel sad? Do you turn to chocolate chip cookies, video games, or scrolling the Internet? We all have different ways of coping with heartache; however, God wants us to turn to him when our hearts are broken. God reminds us that he is close to us when we're hurting. He wants to uplift us when our spirits feel crushed.

One stumbling block that can keep us from finding healing for our broken hearts is getting stuck in feelings of anger toward God. When I was younger, I often allowed anger toward God to turn to bitterness. When the boy I liked rejected me, I didn't do well in a class, or my team didn't win the championship, I blamed my disappointment on God.

Sadly, every time I turned away from God in anger, the pain in my life increased instead of improving. I didn't understand that God wasn't directly trying to make me miserable, and I didn't trust that he was capable of working all situations for good in my life.

Have you ever felt angry that God permitted a tough time in your life? Working through anger is a healthy part of working through losses in life. But it's important not to get stuck in our anger and hold life's disappointments against God. Lingering anger toward God can lead to bitterness, and bitterness will rob us of the joy and peace we long for in life.

If you sense yourself turning away from God in anger, cry out to him and ask him to help you work through the anger instead of getting stuck in it. Talk about the anger with an adult you trust.

God loves you and wants to use this heartbreaking situation for your good and his glory. He also wants to set you free from feelings of sadness and anger.

Girl to Girl:

Life can be tough. You might feel alone and angry that God allowed you to face a difficult loss. You might feel like there is no way out. The truth is, you're not alone!

Jesus died on a cross with nails through his hands and thorns on his head. He endured pain so that we can find healing in him. God loves you, and he will be there for you when times are tough. All you have to do is ask.

"How do you ask?" you might be wondering.

Well, first of all, talk to God about how you feel. He wants you to cast your worries and sadness on him. God also puts people in our lives who can help us work through our difficult feelings. Reach out to a guidance counselor, parent, or trustworthy adult. Talking to a counselor or therapist can be helpful too. God often uses other people to help us heal.

It probably won't miraculously happen right away, but with time, as you seek God, you will realize he is healing your pain.

Talk About It:

- Have you ever been angry with God for allowing pain in your life? How has this anger affected your relationship with God?

- What is the most difficult heartbreak you have ever faced? How did you handle it at the time, and how has God used it to help you grow?

Pray Together:

Jesus, thank you for being our Healer. Help us remember to turn to you in times of heartache and sadness. Help us work through feelings of anger and trust that you are capable of using every difficult situation for our good and your glory. We ask you to reach down from heaven as you heal us with your love. Amen.

Journal Later:

Describe a time in the past when you were heartbroken. What did God use as means to heal your broken heart (friends, hobbies, counselors, parents, prayer, worship, etc.)?

Mom's Reflection:

_____

_____

_____

_____

_____

_____

_____

_____

_____

_____

_____

_____

_____

_____

_____

Daughter's Reflection:

_____

_____

_____

_____

_____

_____

_____

_____

_____

_____

_____

_____

_____

_____

Grumps and Bullies

For the Spirit God gave us does not make us timid, but gives us power, love and self-discipline.

2 Timothy 1:7

Mom's Thoughts:

When I was in middle school, a girl who was once my close friend turned on me. I often caught her glaring at me across the cafeteria or making rude remarks to her friends—just loud enough that I could hear as I walked past her in the hallway.

Losing her friendship hurt. Facing her hurtful comments and angry stares hurt even worse. I wasn't sure how to move on, and every time she looked at me in a mean way, I felt like a dagger was being stabbed into my heart.

Finally, I told my mom about the situation. I'll never forget my mom's advice. She gently reminded me that when people are unkind, it's because something inside of them is hurting. When people act like bullies, it's because they feel broken inside. Being mean to others is the only way they know how to cope with their pain.

My mom's words changed the way I see mean people and bullies forever. I realized that when people are unkind, it's usually not about me at all. It's because something is hurting inside of them.

When someone is mean to you, ask God how to respond. He knows what's happening inside the other person and wants to give you wisdom. You might feel led to ignore the person and walk away, say something kind in response to a mean comment, or firmly stand up for yourself.

We don't have to be close friends with people who are repeatedly mean to us. It's healthy to put up boundaries and not allow unkind people to continue to upset us. However, when someone is unkind, we can remind ourselves that unkind people usually hurt deeply on the inside.

Girl to Girl:

A couple of months ago, I had a problem. We were having a contest at school, and it felt like the teacher was being unfair. The contest required us to participate in class, but I noticed some kids (including me) weren't getting called on. Even worse, the teacher was acting like we weren't participating and giving us a disadvantage in the competition.

The same month, another teacher snapped at me for reading a book while I was just getting organized for the class!

Here's what I tried to remind myself: Even teachers have bad days. If a teacher is rude to you, consider that maybe the teacher isn't feeling well, or maybe something difficult happened at home. The same goes for your friends. Everyone has bad days. When people are mean to you, it's usually because of something that's going on inside of them. Try not to take it personally and remind yourself that people lash out in mean ways because *they* are hurting inside.

Talk About It:

- Have you ever had an experience with a bully or a friend who turned against you? How did you respond?

- It's helpful to remember that people are unkind when they are hurting inside. How might this mentality help you deal with unkind people in different realms of life (rude waitresses, grumpy cashiers, irritated teachers, and even snippy moms)?

Pray Together:

Lord, thank you for giving us a spirit of love, power, and self-discipline. Help us to brush off hurtful words from grumpy people by remembering that people speak unkind words because they are in pain. Show us how to respond to these people as you would respond to them. Amen.

Journal Later:

Write about a time when someone hurt you with their words or actions. How did you respond? What might have been happening within this person at the time?

Mom's Reflection:

_____

_____

_____

_____

_____

_____

_____

_____

_____

_____

_____

_____

_____

_____

_____

_____

Daughter's Reflection:

_____

_____

_____

_____

_____

_____

_____

_____

_____

_____

_____

_____

_____

_____

How We Grow Up

Consider it pure joy, my brothers and sisters, whenever you face trials of many kinds, because you know that the testing of your faith produces perseverance. Let perseverance finish its work so that you may be mature and complete, not lacking anything.

James 1:2-4

Mom's Thoughts:

Jesus was the firstborn in his family, and after he was born, his parents continued to have more children. One of Jesus' brothers was named James, and James didn't always believe Jesus was God's Son. For a while, James merely saw Jesus as his big brother. However, James eventually realized Jesus was the Messiah—the Son of God who came to take the punishment for our sins—and James wrote a book in the Bible.

James knew Jesus in the way brothers know each other. He ate meals with Jesus, lived alongside him, and probably picked fights with him. Listen to what James says about the trials we face in life: "Consider it pure joy whenever you face trials of many kinds!"

I don't know about you, but I don't usually consider it joy when life gets hard. Instead, I'm tempted to complain and grumble. I become passionate in my prayers, and I plead with God to remove the trial from my life!

I'm thankful James teaches us what happens when we face trials. He tells us that the testing of our faith produces perseverance, and perseverance makes us mature and complete.

Do you want to be more of a grownup—mature and complete? Joyfully receive the trials God brings into your life. I sure do wish God would switch things up and use the easy seasons of life to make us mature, but this isn't the way God works. He uses the difficult times in our lives to make us more mature.

The next time life feels hard, remember the words of Jesus' little brother James. God is using your trial to make you mature and complete, lacking nothing!

Girl to Girl:

For a long time, I fought with my brother nonstop. Being mature felt impossible because he picked fights *all the time*! When he picked fights, I would dish it out right back to him, and this led to nonstop bickering. After a while, I realized it was time for me to tone it down.

Sometimes, it feels hard to be mature and walk away from arguments, but I try. I think it's paying off slowly, and sometimes I think about how this might help me in the future. For example, it will help me be patient with my coworkers someday.

God wants to use your troubles to help you become more mature too. He wants to use times of sadness to help you become more compassionate toward people who are sad. He wants to use disappointment so that you can encourage others when they face disappointments. You can trust that God won't waste your tough times. Ask him how you can use your hard times to help others, and he will use your trouble for good!

Talk About It:

- How do you respond when difficult things happen in your life? Do you consider it joy, or do you beg God to take away the difficulty?

- Is any part of your life difficult right now? How might God be using this trial to make you more mature?

Pray Together:

Lord, we thank you for loving us enough to discipline us. Help us find joy and press close to you when we face trials in our lives. We thank you for using our struggles to make us mature and complete. Amen.

Journal Later:

Write about a time in the past when you faced something difficult. Looking back, how did God use your trial to help you become more mature?

Mom's Reflection:

_____

_____

_____

_____

_____

_____

_____

_____

_____

_____

_____

_____

_____

_____

_____

_____

Daughter's Reflection:

_____

_____

_____

_____

_____

_____

_____

_____

_____

_____

_____

_____

_____

God Hears

The Lord has heard my cry for mercy; the Lord accepts my prayer.

Psalm 6:9

Mom's Thoughts:

Have you ever prayed for something for months—maybe even years—and felt heartbroken when God didn't answer the way you hoped? Maybe you were praying for God to heal a loved one, restore your parents' marriage, help you make it onto a team, or bless you with the latest tech gadget. Despite your prayers, nothing seemed to happen. Maybe you decided to give up on prayer.

Most of us will face the dilemma of unanswered prayers.

What do we do when God doesn't answer us—when he doesn't seem to hear us?

First, it's important to stand on the truth we find in the Bible instead of standing on our feelings. It feels like God didn't hear us. However, feeling something doesn't make it true. The Bible tells us that God hears the prayers of his children (see 1 John 5:15). We can stand on this promise.

Believing God hears us can lead to a second troubling thought when our prayers go unanswered: If God hears our prayers, is he ignoring us when he doesn't answer?

The Bible reminds us that our thoughts are not God's thoughts, and our ways are not our ways (see Isaiah 55:8-9). God doesn't often answer our prayers according to our expectations. His thoughts are vastly different than our thoughts. God might not answer our prayers the way we want him to answer, but this doesn't mean he's not listening or that he doesn't love us.

God promises to use all things for the good of those who love him, who have been called according to his purpose (see Romans 8:28). He can take any bad situation and use it for his good purposes. But let's not stop here. The Bible also reveals God's highest and best purpose for any situation: God's ultimate purpose for our trials is to use them to shape us into Jesus' image (see Romans 8:29).

Prayers that seem to go unanswered are often God's way of shaping us to look more like Jesus. While we wait on God, he develops our patience, deepens our trust, builds our compassion, and shapes our hearts into the image of Jesus' heart of love.

Girl to Girl:

It feels like God doesn't hear our prayers when he doesn't answer according to our expectations. Imagine you've been praying for God to heal a loved one, but he doesn't seem to hear. Your loved one continues to get sicker. You pray every single day, but nothing seems to happen. You start to feel like God has abandoned you.

Remember that even when it feels like God isn't working to answer your prayers, he is always working. He often works in different ways than we expect. Maybe he is working to help you trust him more or learn a lesson. Ask him to help you trust him, and rest assured that he hears your prayers!

Talk About It:

- Are you waiting for God to answer a prayer in your life right now? Describe this prayer and share what it would look like for God to answer according to your greatest hopes.

- Describe a time when God didn't answer a prayer but used the situation to help you become more like Jesus.

Pray Together:

Lord God, thank you for hearing our prayers. It's hard for us to understand that our ways are not your ways. Help us trust that when you don't answer our prayers according to our hopes, you are working all things together for our good and your glory. Help us keep soft hearts so that you can shape us into the image of Jesus as we wait on you. Amen.

Journal Later:

Imagine God telling you that you can pick one person in your life to pray for, and you can ask any request for this person. He tells you he will grant your request no matter what it is. Who would you pick, and what would you ask?

Mom's Reflection:

_____

_____

_____

_____

_____

_____

_____

_____

_____

_____

_____

_____

_____

_____

_____

Daughter's Reflection:

_____

_____

_____

_____

_____

_____

_____

_____

_____

_____

_____

Loving Your Body

Do you not know that your bodies are temples of the Holy Spirit, who is in you, whom you have received from God?

1 Corinthians 6:19

Mom's Thoughts:

Do any of your friends ever say mean or critical things about their bodies? Maybe they complain about their hair, their freckles, or their weight. Sadly, many young women have difficulty embracing the bodies God gave them. They compare themselves to others and feel like they are lacking.

God wants us to honor our bodies and care for them as precious gifts. He created us with different bodies because he loves variety. Regardless of the texture of your hair, the shape of your body, the pigmentation of your skin, and the color of your eyes, God calls you beautiful!

As you grow older, some people will put pressure on you to change your body and try to fit into a different image. You might feel pressure to dye your hair, wear lots of makeup, or diet excessively. There's nothing wrong with dying our hair, wearing makeup, and eating healthy foods; however, when we take these behaviors to extremes, they can become the primary focus of our lives. God wants us to live freely, focus on loving him and loving others, and not obsess about our bodies.

Over the past few years, I've been learning to love and care for my body with compassion and kindness. When self-critical thoughts come to mind, I think of someone precious to me. For me, this means I think of Bekah or one of her brothers. I consider everything I adore about these precious young ones, and I let kindness and compassion grow in my heart. Then, I remind myself that God feels these warm and loving thoughts toward me, and he doesn't want me to criticize the body he gave to me.

You might imagine a precious niece or nephew, a younger cousin, or anyone you deeply love. Any time self-critical thoughts come into your mind, think of this person. Would you treat this loved one the way you are treating yourself? If not, use this as a gentle reminder to be kind to the body God gave you.

Girl to Girl:

All over the Internet, you can find people—especially women—complaining about their bodies. Their complaints might make you feel like your body is ugly because you have too many freckles or you feel like you are overweight.

God wants you to know he made you perfect the way you are. After all, the Bible says God made humans in his image. We all look different, and that's what makes us unique. Imagine what life would be like if you, your aunt, your grandma, and your best friend all looked the same, talked the same, and had the same sense of humor. The world would be pretty boring!

One of the biggest ways we can love our bodies is to stop believing that we need to be a certain size to be beautiful. Many girls feel like they can never be thin enough. God wants us to be healthy, and beauty has nothing to do with being thin. I'll leave you with something Mom always says regarding this struggle, and maybe this will help you as well: "It's healthier to carry a little extra weight than to be too thin."

Talk About It:

- Do any of your friends ever complain about their bodies? Do their comments make you feel pressured to change your appearance?

- Are there any parts of your body you don't like—parts you wish you could change? How do you think God sees these parts of you? What would it look like to have a healthy perspective regarding your body—even the parts you don't like?

Pray Together:

God, thank you for giving us these bodies and calling us to serve you with our bodies. The world around us puts pressure on us to look certain ways. Help us to align ourselves with your perspective when it comes to our bodies. Amen.

Journal Later:

If you could change one part of your body, what would you change? What is your favorite part of your body, and why is this your favorite part?

Mom's Reflection:

_____

_____

_____

_____

_____

_____

_____

_____

_____

_____

_____

_____

_____

_____

_____

_____

_____

Daughter's Reflection:

_____

_____

_____

_____

_____

_____

_____

_____

_____

_____

_____

_____

_____

Everybody Has a Boyfriend—Except for Me

For the Lord gives wisdom; from his mouth come knowledge and understanding.

Proverbs 2:6

Mom's Thoughts:

I vividly remember sitting with my first boyfriend on the school bus as we clenched our lunchboxes and talked about our toy car collections. I was sure we'd get married one day and was already brainstorming names for our children. We were in kindergarten.

Not surprisingly, I didn't marry my kindergarten boyfriend. We decided to stick with friendship, and in the long run, being friends was a better decision for us.

Most likely, you know how it feels to have a crush. You catch yourself watching your crush across the cafeteria or during class. You wonder what it would be like to hold hands or receive a Valentine from this special someone.

As you get older, your friends will probably spend a lot of time talking about boys and dating. You might feel pressure to find a boyfriend as well. Believe it or not, your mom has a lot of insight about navigating romantic relationships, and she's probably eager to talk about boys and relationships.

Different families have different boundaries about dating and boyfriends, and your parents might not allow you to have a boyfriend until you're much older. If this is the case, let me assure you that these boundaries are for your good. Most boys aren't ready for this sort of relationship until they are much older. Honoring your parents' boundaries is important, and God will bless you as a result of your obedience.

It's totally normal to have a crush, but let's be honest—you're probably not going to end up marrying the boy you currently have a crush on. This means that if you do decide to become a couple, you will eventually break up, and breakups often ruin friendships. For this reason, if you value your friendship with the boy you like, it's wise to hold off on the romance and continue to build your friendship instead.

Most of all, talk to your mom about boys. She knows much more than she lets on, and her wisdom can help you navigate everything from rejection to how to handle unwanted flirtation.

Girl to Girl:

For a while, there was a boy who liked me. He would do little stunts to impress me. But I was not interested in him one bit. What do you do when this happens? Well, you could try ignoring him and showing him you're not interested. He might get the hint and back off. But sometimes, boys don't get the hint. In this case, you can politely tell him you just want to be friends.

It can be very helpful to find an older friend or trusted adult to give you advice about boys. A guidance counselor, aunt, grandparent, Sunday school teacher, or parent can help because they have all been through the same experience.

My dad always says, "It's best to work on your studies," which is true! You'll find the right boy when it's time. For now, it's good to stick with friendship!

Talk About It:

- How do you feel about having a boyfriend? Do you want a boyfriend right now or not?

- Do you have a crush? Does anyone have a crush on you?

- How much do your friends talk about boys and dating? Do you have questions about the things they are saying?

Pray Together:

God, thank you for designing us to live in companionship with one another. Help us to make wise decisions as we navigate the world of boyfriends and dating. We pray you will help us communicate well and keep talking about this subject. Amen.

Journal Later:

Describe the characteristics of a godly boy or man. Try to name at least five characteristics that do not involve appearance.

Mom's Reflection:

_____

_____

_____

_____

_____

_____

_____

_____

_____

_____

_____

_____

_____

_____

_____

Daughter's Reflection:

_____

_____

_____

_____

_____

_____

_____

_____

_____

_____

_____

_____

_____

_____

Be the Hero

Be kind to one another, tenderhearted, forgiving one another as God in Christ forgave you.

Ephesians 4:32

Mom's Thoughts:

When flawed human beings live within the walls of the same house, people are bound to feel annoyed at times. If you have brothers and sisters, you know exactly what we're talking about. All siblings argue, and it's not easy to zip your lips when you feel irritated. Even if you don't have siblings, you probably know how it feels to be annoyed with your mom, dad, grandparents, or the loved ones closest to you.

How do we handle feelings of annoyance in a godly way?

First, it's important to get into the habit of taking a deep breath and stepping away from tense situations whenever possible. Try to go to a different part of the house, close the door behind you, and put some space between yourself and the person with whom you're not getting along.

Second, a phrase we often use in our house is, "Who is going to be the hero in this situation?"

The hero is the person who does what is right when doing what's right isn't easy. This person offers kindness instead of bickering. The hero is the person who shares the toy, lets the other person eat the last cookie, or gives up the best spot on the couch.

Every day of your life, God will give you opportunities to be the hero in your home. Choose not to engage in the argument, offer kindness instead of anger, and make yourself the hero.

Every time you choose to be the hero, God works in your heart. He shapes you to look a little bit more like the image of Love:

Jesus himself. Keep being the hero, and you will embody the love of Christ.

Girl to Girl:

Imagine you're playing with your little sister and get into an argument about a toy. It's a stuffed animal you've owned for as long as you can remember, and it's special to you. You yell at your sister and snatch the toy out of her hand. She begins to pull at it, nearly ripping it.

After more yelling and more tugging on the toy, your little sister finally lets go and walks away to play with a different toy. You look down at the stuffed animal and suddenly feel immature because you made such a scene over a stuffed toy.

It's normal to disagree with our siblings, but the way we act matters. We always have a choice to either hold our ground or to humbly be the hero. When I hold my ground against my parents or my brothers, it usually doesn't work out well. Being the hero is always the better option.

Talk About It:

- It's hard to "be the hero" in heated moments. Describe a recent argument with a loved one. What would it have looked like for you to be the hero in that situation?

- There is a time to stand up for yourself and a time to humble yourself and put the needs of another person ahead of your needs. Give an example of a time when it would be important to stand up for yourself.

Pray Together:

Lord Jesus, you gave us the ultimate example of "being the hero." While we were still sinners, you laid down your life to pay the price for our sins. Help us embody your love as we go into the world and aim to humbly put the needs of others above our own needs. Amen.

Journal Later:

In what ways would the atmosphere in your home be different if there were never arguments? What is God showing you about your role in these arguments?

Mom's Reflection:

_____

_____

_____

_____

_____

_____

_____

_____

_____

_____

_____

_____

_____

Daughter's Reflection:

Your Talents

Just as a body, though one, has many parts, but all its many parts form one body, so it is with Christ.

1 Corinthians 12:12

Mom's Thoughts:

God gives each of his children unique gifts and talents. You might know what your talents are, or you might feel like you don't have any special talents. Either way, we have good news for you today: God has given you talents and gifts! It often takes time to discover our unique gifts, and our gifts can change with time.

Bekah is gifted at writing, running, drawing, and pretty much everything creative. She also has a compassionate heart, which is displayed when she cares for the animals around our house. She takes care of our pet beagles, cares for her reptile collection, and often saves baby birds and wild orphaned animals. Your mom has been watching your gifts and talents grow for years, and she can offer insight into what she sees as your special talents too.

The most important insight to remember about our God-given talents is this: God wants us to use our talents and gifts for his glory in this world. This might look like using your gift of cooking to bless your family by making dinner. You might use your talent for sports to make friends and talk about Jesus with other kids as you share your love of sports. Maybe you love to sing. You might join the choir at school or church and bless people with your voice.

Scripture reminds us that God wants us to put our whole hearts into everything we undertake—including our gifts and talents (see Colossians 3:23). As you continue to ask God how to use your talents for his glory, he will use these experiences to prepare you for the future and allow you to be his vessel in this world.

Girl to Girl:

Everyone has a talent. You might think you don't have any talents, but if you search hard enough, you can find something you're good at—something that makes you come alive inside! You might have an amazing memory. Maybe you're awesome at putting on makeup, climbing trees, playing the piano, caring for animals, organizing messy spaces, or gymnastics.

Whatever your talent happens to be, God wants you to use it to bring him glory. Here are a few examples: If you have an amazing memory, you might memorize Bible verses to share at church or with your friends. If you are good at styling hair, God might one day lead you to work at a salon and share your faith with customers as you cut their hair. Your talents can give you opportunities to spread God's love wherever you go!

Talk About It:

- Name a few of your talents. (Mom, feel free to add input and share the talents you see with your daughter.) How might God want to use these talents for his glory in your life?

- Brainstorm one way you could bless someone with one of your talents this week and come up with a plan to make it happen!

Pray Together:

God, thank you for giving us each unique gifts and talents and calling us to use these gifts for your glory. We ask you to help us pay attention to the activities that make us feel alive and joyful inside. Show us how to use these passions to help others and give you glory. Amen.

Journal Later:

Describe a time when you were blessed by someone who shared a gift or talent with you (think about your teachers, coaches, mentors, family members, and friends).

Mom's Reflection:

_____

_____

_____

_____

_____

_____

_____

_____

_____

_____

_____

_____

_____

_____

_____

_____

Daughter's Reflection:

_____

_____

_____

_____

_____

_____

_____

_____

_____

_____

_____

_____

_____

_____

_____

_____

_____

_____

Guitars and Pianos

The eye cannot say to the hand, "I don't need you!" And the head cannot say to the feet, "I don't need you!"

1 Corinthians 12:21

Mom's Thoughts:

I would love to be musically talented. I wish I could carry a tune, play the guitar, and pound out ballads on the piano. Much to my disappointment, God did not bless me with musical abilities.

I spent years wishing I had musical skills and feeling envious of friends who were good at singing, dancing, and playing musical instruments. Finally, God showed me that he wasn't calling me to be a musician. I realized I could continue trying to painstakingly learn to play various musical instruments, or I could let go of my dreams for musical stardom and embrace my God-given talents.

Life has been much more peaceful since I stopped trying to be someone God didn't design me to be.

The same is true for each of us. It's easy to look at the talents of others and wish we could run as fast, paint as well, or sing as beautifully. However, God has designed us with unique abilities, and he's not asking us to compare ourselves to others and try to be more like them.

In our previous reading, we talked about the talents God has given to you. Today, I'd like to gently point out that it's okay you're not amazing at every skill in the world. Your adolescent years are a wonderful time to explore and discover your talents but don't be too hard on yourself when you realize you're not good at everything. Embrace the gifts God has given you and remember that his plan for you is unique. He will help you fulfill his plan, and his plan will not involve looking like someone else.

Girl to Girl:

For a while, I also wanted to pursue music. As you know, I was in the band at school, and I realized I didn't enjoy it. I was sad because I thought I'd be good at it without lots of practice. I now realize that it wasn't realistic to expect that I'd be a master musician without practice. Most of the time, we need to practice if we want to improve at any skill.

Maybe you want to be an artist, but you can't even draw a stick figure. Or maybe you want to do gymnastics but can't do a cartwheel correctly. It's okay not to be talented in every area. You can either practice to improve your skills, or you can try something new!

Most of all, remember that God wants to use the talents he has given *you*, and he's not asking you to be someone you're not!

Talk About It:

- If you could have one new talent, which talent would you choose?

- Some talents grow with practice. Describe an area of your life in which God might be calling you to keep practicing a skill or talent instead of giving up on it.

Pray Together:

God, we thank you that you don't make mistakes. It's easy to look around and wish we had the gifts and talents we see in other people, but we know that you create us each uniquely for your purposes. Help us embrace the talents you have given us and not be envious of the gifts we see in others. Amen.

Journal Later:

For this journaling exercise, we are going to share the talents we see in one another. Mom, write to your daughter and name at least three talents you see in her. Daughter, write to your mom and share at least three talents you see in her. Gifts and talents might include hobbies and special skills like creativity, artistry, craftiness, or athleticism, or they might be character traits like compassion, kindness, patience, love, thoughtfulness, humor, humility, and joy.

Mom's Reflection:

_____

_____

_____

_____

_____

_____

_____

_____

_____

_____

_____

_____

_____

Daughter's Reflection:

When You Fail

He who began a good work in you will carry it on to completion until the day of Christ Jesus.

Philippians 1:6

Mom's Thoughts:

I vividly remember the first test I ever failed. I was in fifth grade, and the test required us to use alphabetic skills to quickly determine the location of words in the dictionary. I was a good student and was embarrassed that my alphabetic skills were lacking. The failure felt like a looming cloud that followed me around for several days and caused me to feel horrible about myself.

I've never met anyone who enjoys the feeling of failure. Failure hurts. Whether it's a failed test, a mistake during a performance, or feeling like we've disappointed others, it doesn't feel good to fall short.

Some people spend their whole lives running from failure. They avoid taking risks and rarely step out to try new endeavors. Sadly, they are missing out!

You'll face more than a few failures in your life too. We all fail, and failure is an important part of learning and growing. The most important part of the process is not whether we fail (because we all will at times) but how we respond to failure.

Do we let failure lead us to give up?

Or do we get back up and keep trying?

I'll never forget a story my favorite college professor shared in class one day. She told us the story of the first exam she failed as a college student. The failure was crushing, and she was sure her future was ruined.

As she reflected on her failure years later with us, she offered insight that went something like this: "It was just an exam. Everybody fails sometimes. Your future is not ruined if you fail one test or make a mistake. Today's mistakes usually aren't as big of a deal as they seem to be." Her insight took the pressure off my perfectionist personality and debunked the lie that I was somehow capable of destroying God's plan for my life.

The next time you fail a test or mess up in a way that feels awful, remember this: Failure does not define you. You are a child of God, and God will fulfill his purpose for your life. Additionally, the failure that feels huge right now probably won't feel huge in a few short years.

Girl to Girl:

Our dog once gave birth to a litter of nine puppies. We were so excited. Sadly, our excitement turned to sorrow when the puppies began to pass away. We tried everything to save them, but nothing worked. After a week, we were left with only one little puppy.

In some ways, I felt like I failed. I wondered if I could have done something to save them.

At the time, it felt like the world was going to end. Looking back now, I realize God was giving me an opportunity to trust him. He showed me that sometimes, we can give our best effort and things still don't turn out the way we hope. We should never let the fear of failure stop us from trying.

Our family isn't giving up on raising puppies. We're planning to try for another litter of puppies next spring!

Talk About It:

- Describe a time when you failed and felt defeated by the failure. Does this failure still bother you, or have you moved on? What does God want to show you about this situation?

- In what way do the words of Philippians 1:6 take the pressure off of you when it comes to being perfect?

Pray Together:

Lord, thank you that no failure is too great for you to use and redeem. Thank you for using our failures to shape us and help us become mature. Help us trust you and not fear failure as we remember that most growth requires failure along the journey. Amen.

Journal Later:

What dream would you chase if you knew you would not fail? Why haven't you chased it, and what is God revealing to you?

Mom's Reflection:

_____

_____

_____

_____

_____

_____

_____

_____

_____

_____

_____

_____

_____

_____

Daughter's Reflection:

_____

_____

_____

_____

_____

_____

_____

_____

_____

_____

What's on Your Screen?

I will not look with approval on anything that is vile.

Psalm 101:3

Mom's Thoughts:

What's your favorite TV show or series? With the wide array of choices, it's not hard to find an entertaining series and get hooked.

A few years ago, I got into the habit of watching a crime-solving show on TV every afternoon. I was pregnant and not feeling well, and watching TV was the best way to distract me from feeling sick. Because we have limited TV options in our house, I had to choose between soap operas and the crime-solving show. The crime show won.

About a week after I started watching the show, I started having horrible dreams about murders and dead people. After several nights of bad dreams, I realized I needed to quit watching the show. The show didn't make me feel afraid or disgusted when I watched it during the day, but through the dreams, God showed me that the focus on evil was negatively affecting my mind.

In the same way, you might not think it's a big deal that the show you love includes some swearing, immodesty, bullying, immorality, or other ungodly behavior. However, we have to be careful about what we put into our minds. Our entertainment choices influence our thoughts and behaviors.

When we repeatedly watch people living in ways that dishonor God, we get used to this sort of behavior. Once it becomes normal, it's easy for us to slip into the same patterns. You might not have nightmares, but sooner or later, you'll be influenced by the entertainment you choose.

One insight that helps our family determine what to watch on TV comes from Philippians 4:8, which reads, "whatever is true, whatever is noble, whatever is right, whatever is pure, whatever is lovely, whatever is admirable—if anything is excellent or praiseworthy—think about such things." If the show isn't true, noble, right, pure, lovely, admirable, excellent, or praiseworthy, we turn it off. This goes for everything from children's cartoons (which can be surprisingly unpraiseworthy) to the shows we watch together as a family in the evenings.

Girl to Girl:

It's important to be aware of what we're watching. Watching inappropriate shows can change how we think, and we might not even realize it. Shows featuring magic are a good example. These shows portray people casting spells, speaking curses, and acting like witches. These shows seem cool, but if we start to believe in dark magic, we are buying into something that doesn't come from God.

Other shows are less obvious. Watching shows with people who are rude to others can cause us to start being rude to others without even realizing we're doing it. We might pick up habits like swearing or being sarcastic all the time.

This doesn't mean we can only watch baby stuff and cooking shows, but it is important to be careful that we honor God with everything we put on our screens!

Talk About It:

- Does your family have any rules about what you are allowed to watch? How do you feel about these rules?

- Have you ever noticed that a show or video game changed your thoughts or actions? Was it a positive or negative change? What is God showing you about your entertainment choices?

Pray Together:

God, we thank you that you love us and want to protect us. We ask you to help our family honor you with our entertainment choices. Guide us in setting boundaries and deciding what we will and will not watch on our screens. Help us be patient and kind to one another as we navigate this tricky territory. Amen.

Journal Later:

What is your favorite TV show, movie, or series? Why do you like it, and what kind of thoughts does it lead you to dwell on after you watch it?

Mom's Reflection:

_____

_____

_____

_____

_____

_____

_____

_____

_____

_____

_____

_____

_____

_____

_____

_____

Daughter's Reflection:

_____

_____

_____

_____

_____

_____

_____

_____

_____

_____

_____

_____

_____

_____

A Bright Future

Keep this Book of the Law always on your lips; meditate on it day and night, so that you may be careful to do everything written in it. Then you will be prosperous and successful.

Joshua 1:8

Mom's Thoughts:

I was about 12 years old when I decided that my goal in life was to be successful. In my mind, success looked like a big, beautiful home in the country, a happy family, and enough money to feel comfortable.

A decade later, I realized that God's idea of success didn't align with my childhood ideas. As I read the Bible, I didn't see anything about pursuing comfort. I also realized that a big house and a happy family aren't always part of God's plan for our lives. Instead, Scripture tells us to lay down our lives for others. Jesus teaches us to deny ourselves, take up our crosses, and follow him.

So much for my dreams of success and prosperity.

Looking back on my 12-year-old dreams, I see that some of my hopes came to life. God has blessed me with a wonderful husband and three precious children. We have enough money to take care of our needs. Our house isn't exactly big, but we all fit in it, and it's almost in the country.

You might have dreams for your future too. I encourage you to keep dreaming! However, while you dream, remember that the way to find success and prosperity is to stay connected with God. Keep reading your Bible, praying, going to church, and reading books like this one. As you keep seeking him, God will bless you and direct you.

Most likely, your life won't unfold the way you expect. But if you keep pursuing God, hide his Word in your heart, and make him first in your life, the adventure ahead of you will be epic.

Girl to Girl:

Throughout my life, I've had many ideas about what I want for my future. In kindergarten through second grade, I wanted to be a vet. In third grade, I wanted to be a chef. In fourth and fifth grade, I didn't know what I wanted to be.

I'm in sixth grade as I write this to you today, and right now, I want to be a pediatric nurse. Of course, what I want to do may change as I get older, but one thing won't change: I plan to keep seeking God. I know that if I keep seeking him, he will guide me each step of the way!

Talk About It:

- What do you hope for when you think about your future? How do you feel when you think about the future? Are you excited, scared, uncertain, nervous, or something else?

- In addition to reading this book together, what one step can you take, as mother and daughter, to be more consistent about spending time in God's Word? (Consider memorizing a verse together each week. The verses in this devotional would work well! Or you might read a Psalm every day or begin reading through the Bible together at your own pace.)

Pray Together:

Lord, thank you for your promise to guide and direct us. Thank you that your Word renews our minds and guides our lives. We ask you to continue to transform us through the power of your Word and help us follow you in all we do. We trust that when our big dreams for the future are from you, you will bring them to pass in your timing. Amen.

Journal Later:

If you could have three wishes granted for your future, what would you wish for?

Mom's Reflection:

_____

_____

_____

_____

_____

_____

_____

_____

_____

_____

_____

_____

_____

_____

_____

_____

Daughter's Reflection:

_____

_____

_____

_____

_____

_____

_____

_____

_____

_____

_____

_____

_____

God Talks to Us

*Call to me and I will answer you and tell you great and
unsearchable things you do not know.*

Jeremiah 33:3

Mom's Thoughts:

When you pray, do you do most of the talking, or does God add
to the conversation? Most of us approach God with our
concerns, ramble through our lists of needs, and leave no space
for God to speak to us.

You probably have at least one friend who is a good talker but
isn't very good at listening to you. How does it make you feel
when this friend goes on and on about her life and then walks
away without asking you how you're doing?

I sometimes feel frustrated when friends treat me this way. God
is patient with us, and he extends plenty of grace to us. I don't
believe he gets mad at us when we don't create space to listen to
his quiet voice, but I do know that he wants us to learn to hear
his voice.

Jesus offers the following encouragement about listening to his
voice: "My sheep listen to my voice; I know them, and they follow
me" (John 10:27).

God is relational. He wants you to ask him questions and wait to
receive his answers. He wants to give you wisdom and fill you
with his love.

You can practice listening to God at the beginning of every day
by starting your day with this question: "Lord, what do you want
me to know as I follow you today?" Ask this question before you
get out of bed in the morning and wait for God to put an
impression upon your heart.

I ask this question often. God often responds by putting a loved one on my heart, reminding me to be gentle with my children, putting a Bible verse in my mind, or reminding me of how much he loves me. It's important to note that God always directs our thoughts in accordance with Scripture. He leads us in ways that are loving toward us and loving toward others.

Make it a habit to ask God what he wants you to know about your problems, your concerns, and your days. He is waiting to guide and direct you. We'll talk more about hearing God's voice in our next two readings!

Girl to Girl:

There are many ways to communicate with God. Each morning before the day starts, everyone in our family takes turns thanking him for one gift, and then we each name something we need help with. Sometimes we rest and ask God to join us, as I described earlier in this devotional. Often, God speaks to us during these times.

We can also talk to God by asking him questions. He might not answer right away, but as we watch for him, he will show us what to do and give us wisdom.

God wants to talk to each of us. It's up to us to make sure we're listening!

Talk About It:

- How do you feel when a friend rambles on about her life and never asks about your life? Why is it important to create space to listen for God to speak?

- Take a moment to pause and individually ask God what he wants you to know as you follow him through the rest of your day (or what he wants you to know for tomorrow if you are reading this before bed). Quietly listen for any impression on your heart and share what you sense he might be showing you. We'll learn how to test our impressions in the next two readings.

Pray Together:

God, thank you for speaking to us! We want to create more space to listen to your voice. Help us honor you with our prayers, our words, our attitudes, our actions, and our lives. Amen.

Journal Later:

Name a problem you would like God to help you solve. Ask him what he wants you to know about this problem and write anything that comes to mind in the space below.

Mom's Reflection:

_____

_____

_____

_____

_____

_____

_____

_____

_____

_____

_____

_____

_____

_____

_____

_____

_____

Daughter's Reflection:

_____

_____

_____

_____

_____

_____

_____

_____

_____

_____

_____

What Does God's Voice Sound Like?

Whether you turn to the right or to the left, your ears will hear a voice behind you, saying, "This is the way; walk in it."

Isaiah 30:21

Mom's Thoughts:

I've spent decades learning to discern God's voice, and I find it astounding that the Creator of the universe wants to talk to little old me!

You might be reading these words and imagining a deep, booming voice echoing from heaven. Occasionally, people report hearing God's audible voice; however, God doesn't usually speak in a voice we can hear with our ears. Instead, he speaks through the Bible, subtle impressions, circumstances, and even other people!

God most reliably speaks to us through his written Word. He gave us the Bible to direct us, reveal his love to us, and help us understand his character. When I need wisdom, I turn to the Bible first, and I often find an answer within its pages.

In addition to speaking through the Bible, God often speaks to us through subtle impressions. We have a deep sense of "knowing" which decision to make, or we have sudden wisdom about how to handle a difficult situation. God's impressions often bring a deep sense of peace and refreshment—like a cool breeze on a warm summer day.

God also speaks through circumstances. For example, when he is about to redirect my life, I usually start to feel restless. I sense it's time for a change, and I start praying and watching for God to open doors of opportunity. The open doors of opportunity are often God's way of speaking through our circumstances.

Lastly, God can use other people to speak to us. It's important to have older, wiser believers in our lives to help direct us. God has used coaches, teachers, mentors, pastors, friends, and even my kids to speak to me. He wants to speak to you through the people in your life too!

It's important to note that we can easily mistake our desires for God's voice. We can get it wrong. For this reason, it's important to test the impressions we receive to determine whether we're really hearing from God. We'll talk more about this in our next devotion!

Girl to Girl:

A few years ago, I caught two turtles and kept them in a tank in my room. I loved watching them. They were so interesting and cool. They were also smelly, and I couldn't play with them.

As time went on, I didn't want to let them go, but I also knew they belonged in the wild. God didn't talk to me directly, but he gave me a deep sense that I needed to set them free.

After we returned the turtles to the wild, I knew it was the right move. I could tell they were happier the minute they swam into the deep, swampy water. When we left the woods that day, I was sad that my turtles were gone, but I also had the peace that comes from knowing God had directed me and I had obeyed his voice!

Talk About It:

- Do you ever sense God speaking to you? If so, what do you sense him telling you? If not, how do you feel about hearing from him?

- Ask God to bring to mind an example of a time in your life when he spoke through circumstances—showing you something that you just knew you needed to do. Describe what happened.

Pray Together:

Father, thank you for your desire to speak to us. Help us learn to listen to your voice as we make decisions and go about our days. We are honored that you love us so much that you want to guide us. Amen.

Journal Later:

If you could ask God one question and receive an answer, what would you ask him? Why would you ask him this question, and what do you hope he might show you?

Mom's Reflection:

_____

_____

_____

_____

_____

_____

_____

_____

_____

_____

_____

_____

_____

_____

_____

_____

Daughter's Reflection:

_____

_____

_____

_____

_____

_____

_____

_____

_____

_____

Wait, Was That God?

But the wisdom that comes from heaven is first of all pure; then peace-loving, considerate, submissive, full of mercy and good fruit, impartial and sincere.

James 3:17

Mom's Thoughts:

We talked about hearing God's voice in the previous devotion. I mentioned the importance of testing whether we're hearing from God. It's easy for our strong emotions to get in the way and lead us to miss God's voice.

Today, let's talk about five sources that can help us determine whether we're hearing from God: 1.) Scripture, 2.) common sense, 3.) wisdom, 4.) mature believers, and 5.) the test of time. Let me elaborate.

First, when trying to determine whether you're hearing from God, begin by turning to Scripture. God will never lead you to do something that does not align with the Bible's teaching and his character as portrayed in the Bible.

Second, God gave us common sense. Does the thought you are receiving align with basic common sense? If not, there's a good chance it's not coming from God.

Third, like common sense, God gives us wisdom. His direction is always wise, and his voice is always filled with wisdom. Does your thought seem wise or foolish? Answering this question will help you determine whether you're hearing from God.

Fourth, more mature believers will help you determine whether you are hearing from God. I don't make big decisions without first talking to some trusted people who are older and wiser. We were created for community, and a community of wise mentors can help guide you.

Fifth, God's voice stands the test of time. Here is what I mean: Sometimes, I feel really excited about starting something new. I want to start a club, write a book, or buy something that costs a lot of money. Whenever possible, I give these big decisions at least three months before I make a decision.

When my inspiration is truly from God, I still want to pursue the venture after a few months. When it's just my excitement speaking, the excitement usually fades within a few months.

Learning to tell the difference between God's voice and our human thoughts takes time and practice, but God wants to help us. We won't always follow God perfectly, but when we make mistakes, we can trust that he is always able to redirect us back onto the right path.

Girl to Girl:

In our last devotion, I told you about my turtles. Well, when I first realized they needed to move out of my room, my idea was to build a pond for them in our backyard. I was super excited and started saving my money.

After about a month of saving, I realized it would be too much work and too expensive to build a pond. I could make them happier by setting them free in a pond in the woods. (Sidenote: We caught my turtles near home, and they are native to the area. Don't ever release nonnative creatures into the wild!)

Looking back, I see that God was giving me wisdom and showing me the best decision for the turtles and for our family. I didn't hear him speaking to me directly, but he gave me his wisdom. God wants to direct you too. Ask him to guide you, and he will show you what to do!

Talk About It:

- Do you have wise mentors to help you discern God's voice? Besides your mom (of course!), who can you talk to when you need advice?

- Why is it important to test our impressions and determine whether we're hearing from God? What might happen if we claim to hear from God but dishonor him with our actions?

Pray Together:

Lord, thank you for your desire to keep us on the straight and narrow path. We want to learn to listen to your voice and follow you. Help us be wise and discerning as we aim to stay in step with you. Amen.

Journal Later:

Have you ever been excited about something, but after giving it time, you realized you didn't want it as much as it seemed at first? What can you learn from this experience?

Mom's Reflection:

_____

_____

_____

_____

_____

_____

_____

_____

_____

_____

_____

_____

_____

Daughter's Reflection:

_____

_____

_____

_____

_____

_____

_____

_____

_____

_____

_____

_____

Slacking Off

Don't be misled—you cannot mock the justice of God. You will always harvest what you plant.

Galatians 6:7, NLT

Mom's Thoughts:

A few years ago, I had visions to plant and cultivate a flourishing row of wildflowers in the backyard. One cool spring morning, I found a paper bag of seeds I'd been saving for a couple of years. I crawled along the deck and prepared the grassy soil to receive a long row of seedlings—making sure to till up the ground and prepare the earth properly.

As I planted the seeds, I imagined colorful zinnias and asters standing tall in the summer sunbeams. I imagined a rainbow of colors and the joy I would feel while sitting on the deck and admiring the beautiful variety of petals.

Much to my disappointment, days turned into weeks, and weeks turned into months, and no wildflowers emerged through the soil—not even a tiny green sprout. I felt like I'd wasted my time crawling around in the mud, and I was disappointed that my beautiful wildflowers would not be adding joy to my summer days.

A couple of months after planting the seeds, I told my dad about my failed wildflower project.

"How old were the seeds?" he asked.

"I don't know. I'd had them a couple of years," I replied.

"That's the problem," he declared. "You tried to plant old seeds, and they were no longer fertile."

I think of my failed wildflowers from time to time. Just like infertile seeds won't produce a harvest, our lives won't reflect God's glory and goodness if we plant "bad seeds."

Our relationships won't be healthy if we argue and speak mean words. Our grades won't be satisfactory if we don't put forth sufficient effort. We won't excel in athletics if we spend every free moment playing video games or watching TV.

Do you want to see different results in any area of your life? Make sure you're planting the right seeds.

Girl to Girl:

Do you ever feel tempted to slack off? Most of us feel this way from time to time. Maybe you play a sport that you don't exactly love, or perhaps there's a class you don't like at school.

When you don't like something, it can be easy to give less than your best. For example, maybe you only played soccer to see if you would enjoy it, but you soon realized there's way too much running involved! Because you don't enjoy it, you don't give it much effort. Sadly, you're dragging your team down by not trying.

It's important to remember that slacking off never results in good outcomes. You might end up hurting your team or getting a bad grade. You also get into the pattern of not giving your best effort. God always wants us to give our best. Remember that even if you're not loving the assignment in front of you, give your best effort, and you will plant good seeds!

Talk About It:

- Describe a time when you didn't put your whole effort into a task (a school assignment, an afterschool activity, or a project at home). How did the results turn out?

- In which area of your life are you most often tempted to slack off and not give your best effort? What might happen if you don't give your best effort?

Pray Together:

God, thank you for giving us the freedom to influence the direction of our lives. We know you are sovereign over all things, but you also allow us to reap what we sow. Help us to give our best and sow good seeds so that the fruit in our lives will point to your glory and goodness. Amen.

Journal Later:

What is one goal you would like to achieve in the next year? Describe the steps you can take to help you reach this goal.

Mom's Reflection:

_____

_____

_____

_____

_____

_____

_____

_____

_____

_____

_____

_____

_____

_____

_____

_____

Daughter's Reflection:

_____

_____

_____

_____

_____

_____

_____

_____

_____

_____

_____

_____

_____

_____

The War in Your Head

Those who live according to the flesh have their minds set on what the flesh desires; but those who live in accordance with the Spirit have their minds set on what the Spirit desires.

Romans 8:5

Mom's Thoughts:

Does it ever feel like there's a war going on inside you? One part of you knows what's right and wants to honor God, but another part of you wants to act in all sorts of ungodly ways. You might feel ashamed of your desires and temptations. Well, we have good news for you today: You are not alone!

Everyone struggles with temptation. We all feel like there's a war inside our bodies at times. When Jesus walked on this planet, he faced every temptation known to humankind. Your temptations and desires are not sins until you act upon them, and God wants to give you the strength to rise above temptation.

You might struggle with the temptation to lie to your parents or fight with your siblings. Maybe you feel tempted to follow your friends into ungodly behaviors. Regardless of what kind of temptation you face, God has advice to help you overcome your temptations.

God's Word teaches us the difference between the two forces at war within us. One of the forces is called "the flesh." The flesh focuses on what our bodies naturally desire when we're not living in line with God. The good news is that we don't have to be ruled by the flesh. If we know Jesus as our Lord, he has placed his Holy Spirit inside of us. The Bible refers to the presence of God within us as "the Spirit." Yes, the Spirit of God lives inside every believer! The Spirit shows us how God wants us to live.

The war you feel inside is real! You have the power to choose which voice you will follow: the voice of the flesh or the voice of the Spirit!

Girl to Girl:

I feel the temptation to follow my flesh when it comes to fighting with my brother. He might start by saying something rude or hitting me for no reason. I know it's wrong to do the same thing in return, but it can be hard when he puts on a smug face and laughs as he walks away.

How do you win the war inside your head? I've learned to take a deep breath and walk away. I remind myself that my brother wants me to fight. Walking away will make him angry because he didn't get the response he was hoping for. In this way, I kinda feel like I won the battle. I also feel good about myself for doing the right thing.

You probably get frustrated with someone in your life too. It's hard not to smack your sibling when you're angry! Instead, try taking a deep breath and walking away. You will know you did the right thing.

Winning the war in our heads can be tough, but God always provides a solution. Most of the time, we just need to slow down, take a breath, and ask him to show us what to do.

Talk About It:

- Do you ever feel like there's a war between good and evil happening inside you? In what ways does your flesh tempt you to sin most often?

- What would it look like to follow the voice of the Spirit the next time your flesh leads you into temptation?

Pray Together:

God, we thank you for sending your Holy Spirit to live inside our hearts. Thank you for guiding us through the inspiration of your Spirit. Help us rise above the flesh and live to please your Spirit this week. Amen.

Journal Later:

What situations make you feel most tempted to live according to your flesh and act in ways that dishonor God? What is God showing you about relying on the power of the Holy Spirit in these moments?

Mom's Reflection:

_____

_____

_____

_____

Daughter's Reflection:

_____

_____

_____

_____

_____

_____

_____

_____

_____

_____

_____

_____

_____

_____

_____

The Gift You Didn't Ask For

Therefore, in order to keep me from becoming conceited, I was given a thorn in my flesh, a messenger of Satan, to torment me.

2 Corinthians 12:7

Mom's Thoughts:

If you could change one thing about yourself, what would you choose to change? Maybe you have a learning disability, a mental health struggle, a chronic health condition, or a physical trait you dislike. You might get nervous about making new friends or speaking in front of other people. Maybe you've asked God to change you, but he doesn't seem to hear your prayers.

I have weak areas in my life too. Lately, God's been reminding me that these weak areas are the places where he wants to make his power known through me.

Do you feel weak in some realm of your life? God wants to use this part of your life to help others see that we all have weaknesses, and weaknesses don't disqualify us from living for Jesus. God can use your weaknesses to help others see that the heart matters more than what we see on the outside. He can use your struggles to show others that he uses imperfect people for his glory. Your weaknesses don't have to hinder his work in your life.

The Apostle Paul referred to his weakness as a thorn in his flesh. He never described the thorn in specific detail, but we know it tormented him. Whatever his thorn was, we know that the Lord used it to make his power known in Paul's weakness.

Like Paul, you didn't ask for this "thorn," but God can use it for his glory. Ask him to help you trust him. God wants to make his power known and work miracles through your weaknesses!

Girl to Girl:

If I could change anything about myself, I would never get ulcers in my mouth again! You might be thinking, "What's so bad about a few ulcers? Everyone gets ulcers. Plus, they'll go away!"

Looks like it's story time!

When I was about four, the ulcers often covered my whole mouth. I couldn't talk or even eat. I remember going to many doctors as we tried to stop them. The doctors said that the ulcers should stop when I got older. We just needed to wait it out. While we waited, we tried to help the pain with numbing medicines and lots of weird mouth rinses that tasted terrible!

The ulcers aren't as bad as they used to be, but they still come and go. About a year ago, we discovered red light therapy. My grandparents bought an expensive red light to shine on the sores, and we all hoped it would work. The light helps the ulcers heal faster, but I still wish the ulcers would just go away forever.

My point is this: Weaknesses like my ulcers can help make us stronger. The ulcers have helped me have more compassion for other people who suffer from difficult conditions. My "thorn" might even help me be stronger in the future!

I never asked for this, but I try to make the best out of it.

Talk About It:

- If you could change one thing about yourself, what would you change? Do you ever feel limited or feel weak in any way?

- In what ways might God want to use your greatest physical, emotional, or mental limitation for his glory?

Pray Together:

Lord God, you don't make mistakes. You are in control over every realm of our lives. Sometimes, it's hard to understand why you allow limitations and weaknesses in our lives. Help us trust that you let these weaknesses remain so that you can work in powerful ways. Amen.

Journal Later:

If you had to name your greatest weakness, what would you say? What might God want to show others through your greatest weakness?

Mom's Reflection:

_____

_____

_____

_____

_____

_____

_____

_____

_____

_____

_____

_____

_____

_____

_____

_____

_____

Daughter's Reflection:

_____

_____

_____

_____

_____

_____

_____

_____

_____

_____

_____

_____

_____

I'm With the Boss

And God raised us up with Christ and seated us with him in the heavenly realms in Christ Jesus.

Ephesians 2:6

Mom's Reflection:

Do you know what it means to find your identity in Christ? A few years ago, the Lord helped me understand my identity as his daughter in a new way. He taught me this important lesson by reminding me of the way I felt about my dad as a little girl.

When I was young, my dad was a high school teacher. He sponsored a club for high school students dedicated to wildlife conservation. Every year, his club hosted an enormous sportsman's show. The entire high school was filled with wildlife experts, speakers, displays, and even living animals. Thousands of people from the community came to enjoy the show.

I beamed with pride every year as I attended the show. I felt special because my dad was the man in charge. I remember walking through the door and telling the ticket collector that I didn't have to pay because my dad was Bob Miles. "Oh, come right in," the young woman said, clearing the way for me. I felt like a very important person.

Your identity as God's beloved daughter offers you a similar position. You are seated in heavenly places with God himself. He goes before you and behind you. He has anointed you to live on mission with him in the world. Just as my dad was the "boss" of the sportsman's show, God is kind of like the boss of the entire universe. Wherever you go, never forget this truth about your identity in Christ: You are special because your Father is the Boss.

Girl to Girl:

My dad coaches soccer. I don't play soccer anymore, but I help him coach my brother's team. I enjoy seeing my father work with the kids. They have respect for my dad, and it makes me feel special and important because my dad is in charge, and everyone looks up to him.

We should feel this way about God too. He isn't a soccer coach, BUT HE DID CREATE THIS WHOLE WORLD! We are his children, and he loves us. This should make us feel special and important inside. We can be proud that our heavenly Father is the Ruler of all rulers!

Do you ever feel like you're not important or like you don't matter? You matter so much to God that he let his precious Child die in your place. Now, that's love! He is the King of the world, and you belong to him!

Talk About It:

- In what ways would your life change if you learned to enter every intimidating situation with the core belief that you're with the Boss?

- Have you ever felt special because you were connected to someone in an important position of authority? If so, how did this change the way you acted? If not, discuss how it would feel to walk into a busy place and know you were the daughter of the person in charge.

Pray Together:

Father God, we thank you that wherever we go in life, we have the authority to say, "I'm with the King, the Boss, the One in charge," because you rule and reign over every realm of this world. Thank you that you will never leave us. Thank you for covering us with your protection when life is difficult. Help us grasp our identities as your beloved daughters on a deeper level today. Amen.

Journal Later:

Describe a time when you felt special, cherished, and set apart. If you've never felt this way, describe how your life would be different if every time you walked into a room, you remembered that you are with the One who is in charge of the universe.

Mom's Reflection:

_____

_____

_____

_____

_____

_____

_____

_____

_____

_____

_____

_____

_____

_____

_____

_____

_____

Daughter's Reflection:

_____

_____

_____

_____

_____

_____

_____

_____

_____

_____

_____

_____

_____

Worship With Your Life

Therefore, I urge you, brothers and sisters, in view of God's mercy, to offer your bodies as a living sacrifice, holy and pleasing to God—this is your true and proper worship.

Romans 12:1

Mom's Thoughts:

What picture comes to your mind when you hear the word *worship*?

Most of us think about music when we refer to worship. However, Romans 12:1 offers a different take on the familiar word: We are told to offer *our bodies* as living sacrifices, and this is our true and proper worship.

Worshipping God with music can be a joy-filled, powerful, and emotionally riveting experience. God wants us to worship him in song. But God also wants us to learn to worship him with our lives. You worship God with your body every time you deny yourself and put another person's needs above your desires. Here are a few practical examples of what it might look like to worship God with your body:

- You worship God with your body when you resist the sarcastic comment you'd like to make to your sibling.

- You take time out of your busy schedule to call your grandparents or another lonely loved one.

- You put your whole heart into the science project you've been working on.

- You bake a batch of cookies to deliver to an elderly neighbor.

- You help your parents with a chore you don't usually undertake.

- You use a talent to serve a friend.

- You say something kind to someone who looks sad.

These actions don't feel particularly holy or spiritual, but you will strengthen your relationship with God and with others every time you use your body for his glory. This kind of worship delights God's heart.

Girl to Girl:

There are many ways to worship Jesus with our bodies. Every time we share God's love with others, we worship him with our bodies.

When I was younger, I helped Mom make Christmas cookies. We went around to the neighbors' houses in the frigid winter weather and blessed them with our Christmas cookies. They were all quite happy to receive the cookies, and I looked forward to delivering them every year.

God wants us to worship him with our lives by showing the world his love. You might follow the tradition Mom and I started and bake cookies to share with your neighbors or friends. You might worship God with your body by helping an elderly friend rake leaves or do yardwork. Sometimes, our family picks up garbage along the road, and we feel God's joy as we take care of the Earth.

Right now, I am trying to learn how to crochet. I find it pretty cool. I might worship God while I crochet by enjoying the relaxing activity with him or making something to give as a gift.

There are no limits to the ways we can worship God with our lives. The important thing to remember is this: Whatever you do, make it about loving others, and you will worship God with your life!

Talk About It:

- Do you enjoy worshiping God with music? Why or why not?

- What is one way you could worship God using your body sometime in the next week? Come up with a plan and make it happen!

Pray Together:

God, thank you for filling us with your love so that we can pour it out and give it away to others. Show us how we can use our bodies to worship you by serving others this week—and beyond. Help us remember that we glorify you when we step out of our comfort zones to love and serve other people. Amen.

Journal Later:

Every time you bless someone else, God is pleased. Write about a recent time when someone in your life honored God by blessing you.

Mom's Reflection:

_____

_____

_____

_____

_____

_____

_____

_____

_____

_____

_____

_____

Daughter's Reflection:

_____

_____

_____

_____

_____

_____

_____

_____

_____

_____

_____

_____

She Did *What*?

Love does not dishonor others, it is not self-seeking, it is not easily angered, it keeps no record of wrongs.

1 Corinthians 13:5

Mom's Thoughts:

Ava got suspended from school for three days for writing a bad word on the bathroom wall. Adam got caught cheating on Friday's science test, and the teacher ripped up the paper and threw it in the garbage. Meghan has a crush on Joey, but Joey told her to get away from him in gym class yesterday.

These are juicy pieces of information, and it's hard not to spread the news. Throughout most of my life, I had a misunderstanding about the true definition of the word *gossip*. I incorrectly believed that gossip was sharing *false* information. A few years ago, a friend redefined my definition of gossip when she told me that gossip is sharing *any negative* information about others—whether it's true or false.

How are you doing when it comes to keeping negative news to yourself? Today's verse reminds us that love does not dishonor others or keep a record of wrongs. Are you keeping track of the mistakes of others? Do you share their mistakes with your friends?

It's hard not to pass on the news when something scandalous happens. But God calls us to honor others, and this includes protecting them when bad things happen in their lives—even when they get in trouble.

The next time you feel tempted to spread a juicy tidbit of gossip, remind yourself that God wants you to honor others by keeping their failures to yourself. A good rule to live by is this: If you were on the other side of the situation, would you want someone else dishonoring you by spreading the news of your blunder? If not, then extend this same kindness to others and keep their mistakes to yourself.

Girl to Girl:

Last year, a girl in my school got in big trouble and was suspended. In my school, that kind of news travels fast. She was suspended in the morning, and by the end of the day, the whole school knew about it.

Imagine someone in your class did something wrong and got in trouble for it. You're the only person who saw what happened, and you're just dying to tell all your friends about it. Here's a good rule to remember: If someone is in danger, tell an adult what is going on. But if no one is in danger and no one is being hurt, don't spread negative information about others just for fun. This is gossiping.

The next time a friend tells you something bad about someone else, don't spread the gossip—no matter how hard it is!

Talk About It:

- Do your friends spend much time gossiping? Do you find it difficult to avoid joining in? In what sorts of situations are you most tempted to gossip about others?

- Has someone ever spread negative information about you? How did it make you feel?

- Has someone ever protected you by not sharing an embarrassing secret? How did this make you feel?

Pray Together:

Lord God, thank you for your great love for us. You love us so much that you want to show us how to live godly lives of love. We confess that it's easy to fall into gossip. Help us catch ourselves when we're joining in gossip with others. Help us protect and love others by refusing to spread negative information about them. Amen.

Journal Later:

Words of kindness are the opposite of gossip. Think of the kindest words another person has ever spoken to you or about you. What did the person say, and how did these words make you feel?

Mom's Reflection:

_____

_____

_____

_____

_____

_____

_____

_____

_____

_____

_____

_____

_____

_____

_____

_____

Daughter's Reflection:

_____

_____

_____

_____

_____

_____

_____

_____

_____

_____

_____

_____

Bad Habits

No temptation has overtaken you except what is common to mankind. And God is faithful; he will not let you be tempted beyond what you can bear. But when you are tempted, he will also provide a way out so that you can endure it.

1 Corinthians 10:13

Mom's Thoughts:

Do you have any bad habits? Most of us have at least one bad habit. Maybe you bite your nails or play with your hair when you feel nervous. Some bad habits are harmless, but others can hurt you and hurt others.

As you grow older, you'll face more and more temptations to indulge in behaviors that can potentially become bad habits. Throughout my entire life, I've struggled with the bad habit of picking my cuticles—the skin around my fingernails. It's such a deeply ingrained habit that I often don't even realize I'm doing it. If I've had a particularly stressful day, it's not uncommon to get to the end of the day, look at my fingers, and see that my cuticles are sore or even bleeding.

I've been trying to kick this bad habit for decades. I have yet to kick it out of my life for good, but I'm encouraged by today's verse. This verse tells us that God will always show us a way out in moments of temptation. Lately, he's been showing me that I can release stress by keeping a smooth stone in my pocket and rubbing it instead of picking my cuticles. I'm making progress with this bad habit.

God wants to help you overcome your bad habits too. Ask him to show you creative ways to avoid the temptation to indulge in your habit. A replacement activity can be a great way to redirect your attention when you're tempted to indulge in your habit.

What do you love to do? Instead of succumbing to your habit, do the thing you love: Read a book, draw a picture, or take a walk. Ask God to show you how to overcome your temptation, and he will provide a way out. It might take time and practice to kick the habit once and for all, but God will help you move in the right direction.

Girl to Girl:

Most of us have at least a few bad habits. You might have a nervous habit of picking at your skin, or you might be in the habit of getting into trouble with your friends.

Breaking habits can be tough. When it comes to getting into trouble with your friends, you might even feel peer pressure to give into the habits. The good news is that you CAN break these habits!

As my mom shared, finding something else to do instead of indulging in your bad habit can be helpful. Wearing a piece of jewelry and using it as a fidget is a good way to break a habit like picking at your skin. You might encourage your friends to do something fun, like visiting a carnival or going to the park, instead of getting into trouble.

God is waiting to help you overcome your bad habits. Best of all, he promises to always provide a way out of it. Look for the way out, and God will help you find it!

Talk About It:

- Do you have a bad habit you would like to break? Have you tried to break it? How did it work out when you tried to break your bad habit?

- Name five activities you love—activities you could enjoy instead of indulging in an unhealthy habit like excessive screentime, eating junk food, or biting your nails.

Pray Together:

Lord Jesus, thank you for promising us that you will never allow us to be tempted beyond what we can bear. Help us learn to look for the way out of our tempting situations. We trust that your way is always best. Amen.

Journal Later:

If you could change one habit in your life to have a healthier, more godly life, which habit would you change? What replacement activity could you choose to pursue instead of this bad habit?

Mom's Reflection:

_____

_____

_____

_____

_____

_____

_____

_____

_____

_____

_____

_____

_____

_____

_____

_____

Daughter's Reflection:

_____

_____

_____

_____

_____

_____

_____

_____

_____

_____

_____

_____

_____

Three Ways to be Godly

Everyone should be quick to listen, slow to speak and slow to become angry.

James 1:19

Mom's Thoughts:

Who is the godliest person in your life? When you think of godliness, you might think of your pastor, your Sunday school teacher, or a loved one who is especially good at showing care and kindness. Today's verse offers three simple ways you can be godly starting right now: Be quick to listen, slow to speak, and slow to become angry!

These three simple commands can help you embody Jesus wherever you go. First, by being quick to listen, you show others you care. When the people in your life are hurting, usually what they need most is just someone to listen—not someone with all the answers to fix their pain. Listening well is loving well. Be the kind of person who is more interested in listening than adding your input, and you will be the kind of person others are drawn to.

Similar to being quick to listen, godly people are slow to speak. Have you ever noticed that people who talk too much often say foolish things? Wise people weigh their words carefully before they speak. They think about how their words will affect others and what sort of influence they want their words to have.

Lastly, godly people are not easily angered, and when they are angry, they don't sin in their anger. Do you have a short fuse? Do you snap at your siblings and friends when you feel frustrated? Most of us have room for growth when it comes to anger. Ask God to help you be more like him. Ask him to help you become the kind of person who is quick to listen, slow to speak, and slow to become angry.

Girl to Girl:

I'm happy to say that many people in my life are quick to listen, slow to speak, and slow to become angry. I'm so thankful for these loving people!

How do we display these traits? Well, if a friend has a problem and wants to talk about it, don't rush her or interrupt her. I just listen. Most of the time, this is what people need most. If we are always giving answers and advice, we're acting more like Google than a true friend!

Also, it's important to be slow to become angry. For instance, if someone steals from you or admits they did something wrong, don't overreact, yell at them, or tell them how awful they are. Instead, listen and keep a calm expression on your face. Ask God to help you be loving and patient. In these ways, our godly influence will draw others to the Lord!

Talk About It:

- Name someone in your life who is quick to listen, slow to speak, and slow to become angry. How do you feel when you spend time with this person?

- Which of these character traits is the greatest struggle for you: being quick to listen, slow to speak, or slow to become angry? What step can you take today to align yourself with God and move in the direction of godliness?

Pray Together:

Lord Jesus, you set the perfect example of how to live a godly life. Thank you for teaching us how to be more like you. We admit that we cannot do this on our own. We need your grace to work in our lives and accomplish what we cannot do for ourselves. Help us become people who are quick to listen, slow to speak, and slow to become angry. Amen.

Journal Later:

What sorts of situations most often cause you to feel angry? What is God showing you about honoring him in these situations?

Mom's Reflection:

_____

_____

_____

_____

_____

_____

_____

_____

_____

_____

_____

_____

_____

_____

_____

_____

Daughter's Reflection:

_____

_____

_____

_____

_____

_____

_____

_____

_____

_____

_____

_____

_____

_____

Kind and Compassionate

Be kind and compassionate to one another, forgiving each
other, just as in Christ God forgave you.

Ephesians 4:32

Mom's Thoughts:

Compassionate people are good at showing care and concern for others. Do you know whose life on Earth was marked by displays of compassion? Jesus!

The Bible often tells us that Jesus approached others and healed them because he had compassion for them. This is an important example for us to keep in mind. Jesus was compassionate, and he wants us to follow in his footsteps and be compassionate, caring, and concerned for the people in our lives.

When you're having a bad day, you probably have certain friends you talk to—these are the friends who are good at listening, loving you, and cheering you up. Most likely, you also have some friends who aren't good at showing compassion. You might turn to these friends when you want to be silly or have fun, but they're not good at helping you through a hard time.

God wants us to learn to be the kind of friends who are good at showing compassion. Here are three ways to show compassion to others:

First, as we've discussed more than once in this book, be a good listener. Most of the time, people who are hurting just need someone to listen to them. Show care on your face when you listen and validate your friend's feelings.

Second, be willing to extend forgiveness. The last part of today's verse tells us to forgive each other, just as in Christ, God forgave us. One aspect of compassion is a willingness to forgive others when they hurt and offend us. God doesn't want us to keep grudges. Grudges lead to bitterness, and bitterness will eat us away from the inside out.

Third, offer words of encouragement and hope. Compassionate people know how to encourage others. Offer hope to your friends by reminding them that God can turn around any situation. Tell your friends about the hope you have in Jesus. You will point them to a Source of hope that will never fail them.

Girl to Girl:

If you look up the word "compassionate" in the dictionary, you'll find that compassion is showing sympathy and concern for others. We show compassion when we help others feel better or try to cheer them up.

Many of my friends are good at showing compassion when I feel sad. Once, one of my friends hurt my feelings, and I was upset. A different friend showed compassion by encouraging me, listening to me, and hanging out with me. I'm thankful for my friends who are good at listening and who show concern when I'm upset. I want to be this kind of friend too!

The next time you see someone who looks sad or discouraged, show compassion by asking if you can help or if you can listen. We can be compassionate toward people who are angry as well. Usually, when someone seems angry, they are hurting beneath the anger. More than anything, they need compassion!

Talk About It:

- Would you describe yourself as compassionate? Why or why not?

- Today's verse also talks about forgiveness. Do you need to forgive anyone in your life? Are you holding any grudges? What is stopping you from extending forgiveness today?

Pray Together:

Jesus, thank you for showing us how to live lives of love and compassion. Help us follow your example and share your love, compassion, kindness, and forgiveness with others. Amen.

Journal Later:

Describe a time when someone in your life was compassionate toward you—maybe one of your friends when you were upset about something. How did this compassion make you feel?

Mom's Reflection:

_____

_____

_____

_____

_____

_____

_____

_____

_____

_____

_____

_____

_____

_____

_____

_____

Daughter's Reflection:

_____

_____

_____

_____

_____

_____

_____

_____

_____

_____

_____

_____

_____

Let God Lift Your Head

But you, Lord, are a shield around me, my glory, the One who lifts my head high.

Psalm 3:3

Mom's Thoughts:

What makes you feel better in times of sadness? Do you call your best friend, talk with one of your parents, or try to distract yourself with a movie or book?

There's nothing wrong with letting others encourage us and distracting ourselves when we're sad, but God wants us to learn to find comfort in his presence as well.

A couple of years ago, my Grandma passed away. We were very close, and it felt like my heart was torn in two. I missed her so much that I ached inside.

One cold winter morning, shortly after she went to heaven, I sat by the window and watched the morning light ascend through a lilac mist. I was listening to worship music, but I didn't feel like worshiping God. I felt like curling up in a ball and staying in my bed all day.

Instead of crawling back under the covers, I did something brave. I asked God to help me worship him. I imagined him sitting on his throne in heaven. I imagined him looking at me with tears in his eyes and love in his heart. I lifted my hand in praise to him, and I sang along with the worship music.

The most remarkable shift took place in my heart. God's love washed over me. It felt like a river of love was pouring down from heaven and beginning a work of healing in my heart. I knew God was pleased that I chose to worship him with my broken heart.

That moment took place more than two years ago, but I remember it often. God used worship as a first step toward healing my broken heart. I still miss my Grandma, but I have experienced God as the Lifter of my head.

Girl to Girl:

After my great-grandma died, I felt really sad. I missed going to her house and having playdates with her and my cousins. It was like there was a big, empty place in my heart.

One way that I find comfort is to wear a bracelet my great-grandma gave me for my birthday a few years ago. She told me that my great-grandpa gave it to her when they were first married.

I like to wear the bracelet and remember the many fun times we shared together, and God uses the bracelet to help lift my head. Wearing a bracelet doesn't seem like an especially spiritual thing to do, but anything can become spiritual when we pay attention to God's presence with us.

Ask God what you could do to lift your head from your sadness, and he will show you. It probably won't look the same as it looks for someone else, but you can trust that he wants to help lift your head.

Talk About It:

- Do you need God to help lift your head in any areas of your life right now? Describe any situations that are bringing you sadness today.

- What one step could you take to move toward healing in this sad situation?

Pray Together:

Heavenly Father, thank you for lifting our heads in times of sadness. Thank you that when you lived on Earth, you faced pain and sadness, and you understand our feelings. Help us turn to you and experience you as our refuge, shield, and the lifter of our heads. Amen.

Journal Later:

Describe a time when God helped you heal from something sad you faced in your life.

Mom's Reflection:

_____

_____

_____

_____

_____

_____

_____

_____

_____

_____

_____

_____

_____

_____

_____

_____

Daughter's Reflection:

_____

_____

_____

_____

_____

_____

_____

_____

_____

_____

_____

_____

_____

What's Your Cool?

Accept one another, then, just as Christ accepted you, in order to bring praise to God.

Romans 15:7

Girl to Girl:

You may be asking, "Why is the Girl to Girl" section first for our last devotion? Well, the answer is simple: I see girls like you every day, and I want to direct this last devotion straight to the girls. Before you read more, I want you to ask yourself two simple questions:

1. What is your cool?

2. What is your definition of cool?

Feel free to answer out loud or keep your answer in your mind. Now, let's talk more!

At the beginning of the school year, I felt like I needed to wear makeup, dye my hair, or wear something trendy each day to fit in. In my mind, my "cool" meant looking cool.

Picture this: It's your first day of middle school, and everyone is wearing cute outfits and looking amazing. You're wearing baggy clothes, no makeup, and a ponytail. You feel embarrassed—like you don't belong.

But let's stop right here. The truth is that God never asks us to fit into the crowd. Sadly, many of the people surrounding us don't believe in God. They're not walking toward him; instead, they're walking away from him. If we follow them, we're walking away from God.

God made you perfect! Don't try to change yourself. "Cool" isn't a nice outfit or makeup that looks good; instead, it's embracing the way God made you, being real, and letting God's light shine through you!

Mom's Thoughts:

Thanks for taking the lead on this one, Bekah! You might be surprised to hear that moms can relate to everything you wrote as well. As funny as this sounds, I sometimes walk into crowded rooms of women who look glamorous and wonder if I fit in. I want to look pretty and stylish and cool, and I wonder what the other women think about me.

Sadly, when this happens, I'm focused on myself. Instead of focusing on myself, God wants me to walk into new places with an outward focus. He wants me to ask him how I might carry his love into the room. There's nothing wrong with dressing nicely, wearing makeup, dyeing our hair, and presenting ourselves well. But when we let self-focus get in the way of loving the people God places in front of us, we miss out on his best for us.

Today, I'm going walking with some friends. My "cool" is going to look like a baseball cap, jogging shorts, and a T-shirt I've owned for 15 years. I have a feeling my friends won't mind at all.

Talk About It:

- What sorts of characteristics would you use to describe the "cool" people in your life?

- Would you consider yourself cool? Why or why not?

- Do you ever look around and feel like you don't fit in? What is God showing you about shifting your focus to look for other people to love and encourage instead of focusing on yourself?

Pray Together:

God, thank you for designing us each uniquely for your purposes. Help us remember that you haven't called us to fit into the crowd or be "cool." Help us to be who you created us to be as we carry your light and love into the world. Amen.

Journal Later:

Have you ever met someone who was totally cool but not fake about it—someone who was comfortable being real while also being loving and kind? Describe this person. If you've never met someone like this, describe what this person would act like and look like.

Mom's Reflection:

_____

_____

_____

_____

_____

_____

_____

_____

_____

_____

_____

_____

_____

_____

_____

_____

_____

Daughter's Reflection:

_____

_____

_____

_____

_____

_____

_____

_____

_____

_____

_____

_____

_____

Our Last Words—For Now!

Congratulations! You made it to the end of our adventure together. We pray you are closer as a mother and daughter after sharing your thoughts and reading these devotions together. We also pray you are closer to the Lord!

We encourage you to stay in the habit of seeking God together. This would be a great time to commit to reading through the Bible together, or you might try a different devotional book. We recommend *Live in Light* by Melanie Redd and *The One Year Mother-Daughter Devo* by Dannah Gresh. And don't worry; we have plans to publish another mother-daughter devotional for teen girls and their moms in the near future!

You can also connect with us on Stacey's blog. It's called *Encountering God in the Ordinary* at www.staceypardoe.com. Look for a heading called "Girl to Girl" on the main menu at the top of the page. You'll find a link to our *Girl to Girl* mother-daughter devotional blog. You can also sign up for weekly blog posts to appear in your email, and we'll let you know when our next book hits the market!

Most of all, we pray that you continue to pursue Christ with all your heart. Life is a journey filled with mountaintops and valleys. Pressing into Jesus' presence makes the mountaintops sweeter and the valleys brighter. He wants to be your Living Hope. Be blessed as you continue to pursue him!

Love,

Bekah and Stacey

Acknowledgements

Before we go, we would like to thank everyone who helped us bring this book to life. Melanie Redd, thanks for the phone call on that sunny Monday afternoon. Your encouragement inspired us to make this happen! Mom (Grandma), Beth Husband, and Courtney McNamara, thank you for your editing help and wise insights. Jaime Wiebel, we are grateful for your brilliant cover design and for putting up with so many emails from us. Sarah, Deb, Kelly, and Melanie, thank you for endorsing our words and believing in us! Kelly Haux and everyone who serves our children at Grove City Alliance Church, we especially thank you for your years of faithful leadership in our local church community and for helping Bekah grow into the young woman she has become.

Stacey and Lexi Shannon, thank you for your mother-daughter shared journal, *Connecting with Grace*. This journal prompted Bekah to make sure our book had a journaling section as well!

We wish we could personally hug everyone who supported us on the launch team as well as everyone who has prayed us through this writing journey. You know who you are, and your friendship and support mean the world to us!

Darrell, Caleb, and Aiden, thanks for offering us the space to write. Thanks for believing in our efforts. Grandma and Grandpa Miles, thank you for encouraging us, helping us find time to write, and supporting us in countless ways. Grandma and Grandpa Pardoe, thank you for sharing our writing faithfully, loving us, and believing in us.

Most of all, we humbly thank our Father in heaven for his provision and guidance. Lord, we thank you for helping us trust you, even when we don't understand your ways. Your ways are always higher and better than our ways.

Made in the USA
Las Vegas, NV
06 December 2024

13490468R00144